1009

One-line factoids, bizarre truths and juicy chunks of wisdom

H Chaffey-Millar

ISBN: 9798304773478

DEDICATION

To Yelena and Eithan

No time to read a whole book? Can't even finish a page? No problem! This book of one-liners is for you.

Whether you are looking for some quality lavatory literature or merely seek a gentle reminder that you haven't fully understood the world (yet), you have come to the right place!

Much of the material in this book isn't self-explanatory. May it serve as the start of your own deeper investigation!

1009

The number 1009 is the first 4-digit prime number. It is also a lucky number and a Chen prime. A lucky number is one generated through a particular sieve process and a Chen prime is a prime number p such that p+2 is either a prime or semiprime.

Food Industry

Nanotechnology is used in the food industry for enhancement purposes such as improving flavors, providing health benefits, and increasing the shelf life of products.

Jerusalem Syndrome

Some visitors to Jerusalem experience intense religious-themed delusions, believing they are biblical figures or have a divine mission.

Snoop Dogg's True Phobia

Despite his chill persona, Snoop Dogg has a surprising fear of horses.

Fregoli Delusion

The sufferer believes that different people are, in fact, a single person who changes appearance or is disguised, causing confusion in social interactions.

Ramadan's Moving Dates

Ramadan, the month of fasting, is observed based on the lunar calendar, causing it to shift by about 10 days earlier each solar year, thus accommodating various seasons over the decades.

The Motorized Ice Cream Cone (2004)

A spinning cone designed to lick your ice cream for you. Though quirky, many found it unnecessary, and it melted into obscurity.

Aardvark to Zebra

New Zealand is one of the few countries in the world that doesn't have any native land mammals. The only native mammals are bats, with birds traditionally filling many ecological niches that mammals typically occupy in other parts of the world.

Lake Baikal's Age and Depth

Lake Baikal in Siberia is not only the world's deepest lake, plunging to around 1,642 meters (5,387 feet), but it's also the oldest, estimated to be about 25 million years old.

One-line factoids, bizarre truths and juicy chunks of wisdom

Olympic Controversy
During the Beijing 2008 Olympics, fireworks were so meticulously orchestrated and computerized that some sequences included CGI effects during the live TV broadcast to enhance the viewers' experience.

Zoroastrian Sky Burials
Zoroastrians traditionally practiced "sky burials," where the deceased were placed atop Towers of Silence to be consumed by vultures, thus avoiding contamination of earth or fire.

RBC Rally
If all of your blood vessels were laid end to end, they would circle the Earth approximately two and a half times.

Self-Driving Cars in the 1920s
The concept of self-driving cars dates back to the 1920s when experiments were conducted with driverless cars controlled by radio signals.

Fruit Battery
It's possible to generate a small amount of electricity using common fruits like lemons or potatoes in a homemade battery. The acid in these fruits acts like an electrolyte.

Panda Diplomacy
China has long practiced "panda diplomacy" by gifting or lending pandas to other countries as a means of fostering diplomatic relations.

Babylonian Hepatoscopy
The Babylonians were adept at hepatoscopy, a form of divination where the liver of a sacrificed animal, often a sheep or an ox, was inspected for omens and messages from the gods. They even had clay models of livers as guides.

Passover Giraffe
There is no specific prohibition against eating giraffe in terms of kashrut. It's kosher because it has cloven hooves and chews its cud, though it's not commonly consumed.

Sweat Glands

Dogs primarily regulate their body temperature through panting, as they only have sweat glands in their paw pads. Cats also have sweat glands in their paws, but they groom themselves to cool down with saliva evaporation.

Gustav Mahler's Superstition

The legendary composer Gustav Mahler had a fear of being the ninth in line to die, a superstition stemming from the fact that many composers died after their ninth symphony. He tried to circumvent this by calling his ninth symphony "Das Lied von der Erde (The Song of the Earth)", but he succumbed to his fear and died shortly after completing his official Ninth Symphony.

Giant Eggs

The extinct Moa, a native flightless bird, laid eggs up to 10 times bigger than those of an ostrich!

Floating Solar Farms

In some countries with scarce land resources, solar farms are being constructed on bodies of water, utilizing floating solar panel technology to produce clean energy.

Preservation of Saints

In incorruptibility, certain saints' bodies are said to resist normal decay as a sign of holiness. St. Bernadette Soubirous is perhaps the most famous example; her body remains largely uncorrupted since her death in 1879.

Princely Eye Keepers

Some Chinese emperors from the Ming Dynasty had designated officials whose sole responsibility was to protect the emperor's concubine from getting too close to others and from amorous advances!

Home to a Glacier That Plays Songs

The Ross Ice Shelf has a natural "melody" phenomena where the vibrations of the glacier create a sound reminiscent of a didgeridoo when wind blows across its surface.

One-line factoids, bizarre truths and juicy chunks of wisdom

Zoroastrian Dualism
The Avesta, the holy book of Zoroastrianism, is structured around the dualism of good and evil, including cosmic battles between Ahura Mazda and Angra Mainyu, which influenced later Abrahamic traditions.

Zombie Ants
Some parasitic fungi from the genus *Ophiocordyceps* can control the behavior of ants. They infect the ant's brain, forcing it to climb to an elevated location and secure itself there before the fungus eventually kills the ant and grows its fruiting bodies out of the ant's head to release spores.

Numeric Structure
The Torah contains significant numeric patterns, including numerous references to the number seven, which traditionally denotes completeness and divine order in Jewish scriptures.

Sky Burials in Tibet
The Tibetan practice of sky burial involves leaving the deceased on a mountaintop to decompose naturally or be eaten by birds. This practice is rooted in the Buddhist belief in the circle of life and the impermanence of the body.

Queen Elizabeth II's Eccentric Hobbies
Known for her formality and royal duties, the Queen was also a car mechanic during WWII and kept driving well into her 90s.

Holy Land Replica
In the 19th century, a small group of settlers in Wayne County, Ohio, tried to recreate the geography of the Holy Land in America complete with Mount Zion, Nazareth, and the Jordan River.

Koro Syndrome
Predominantly reported in parts of Asia, this acute anxiety condition involves a belief that one's genitals are retracting into the body, potentially leading to death.

Epic Panegyric

Poetry can be an act of extreme dedication or flattery, as shown by authors who wrote epic-length poems praising patrons, uniquely combining narrative storytelling with intense admiration.

Kumbh Mela

The Hindu Kumbh Mela festival is the world's largest religious gathering, attracting tens of millions of pilgrims to bathe in sacred rivers for spiritual purification and blessings.

Mosque Architecture

Not all mosques have domes and minarets; styles vary widely depending on cultural influences, such as pagoda-like mosques in China and others that incorporate modern designs.

Invisible Color

Butterfly wings are created at the nanoscale and rely on structural color rather than pigmentation. This is why their colors can appear iridescent and change depending on the angle of light.

Actual Time Travel

Due to its position at the South Pole, Antarctica technically operates in every time zone. However, research stations use the time zones of their home countries or logistics partners.

Ancient Grain Vaults

The oldest known granaries date back to around 11,000 years ago in the Middle East, suggesting that humans stored grain even before the full development of agriculture.

Post-it Note Mistake

The adhesive used on Post-it Notes was originally a failed attempt at creating a strong adhesive. Spencer Silver, a 3M scientist, developed a "low-tack" adhesive that was initially disregarded but later became a household staple.

Hawking Radiation

Black holes can slowly evaporate by emitting radiation, known as Hawking radiation. This phenomenon results from quantum effects near the event horizon.

One-line factoids, bizarre truths and juicy chunks of wisdom

Tinkering Schools

Schools like Tinkering Schools allow children to build, create, and experiment using real tools and materials, based on the idea that hands-on experience is a powerful learning method.

Kosher Tequila

Many people are surprised to learn that some tequila brands are certified kosher. This involves close monitoring of the production process to ensure no non-kosher substances contaminate the beverage.

Nykur's Temptation

In Icelandic folklore, the Nykur or Nixie is a water spirit that takes the form of a horse-like creature. It lures people onto its back and then drags them into the water to drown them. It can be thwarted by saying its name aloud, causing it to lose its power.

Uncountable Reals

The set of real numbers is "uncountably infinite," meaning they cannot be listed in a way that matches them with natural numbers, as demonstrated by Cantor's diagonal argument.

Silent Beginnings

Thomas Edison believed that silent films would be commercially viable forever and insisted on producing films without sound, considering it a mere novelty.

Rhino Horn Infusion

Some conservationists inject rhino horns with dye and an anti-parasitic chemical to make them worthless on the black market. The process doesn't harm the rhinos but deters poachers.

Etruscan Bronze Liver

The Etruscans practiced divination, reading omens from animal livers. An artifact known as the "Liver of Piacenza," a bronze model of a sheep's liver, was used for teaching augury, mapping celestial bodies to the organs.

Underwater Vehicles of World War II

During WWII, the German military invented an underwater bicycle to allow divers to travel longer distances beneath the surface quietly.

Information Paradox

Black holes may hold the key to solving the "information paradox," a mystery about whether information that falls into a black hole can be completely lost, conflicting with principles of quantum mechanics.

Streaming Beginnings

Netflix actually began as a DVD rental service by mail in 1998 and only introduced streaming services nearly a decade later, in 2007.

Dada Poetry

During the Dada movement, poets would create "chance poems" by cutting words from a newspaper, throwing them into a bag, and pulling them out randomly to dictate the order.

Microdoses of Electricity

The human brain generates about 20 watts of electricity, enough to power a dim light bulb. This electrical activity is essential for sending signals between neurons.

The Dimple Maker (1936)

Promoted for facial beauty, this device claimed to create dimples by applying pressure to the cheeks. The awkward appearance and discomfort ensured it never caught on widely.

The Rendlesham Forest Incident

In December 1980, U.S. Air Force personnel stationed at RAF Woodbridge in England reported encountering strange lights and a UFO in Rendlesham Forest, leading it to be dubbed "Britain's Roswell."

Shrinking Icebergs with Bacteria

Some Antarctic icebergs are melting from beneath due to microorganisms that generate heat, leading to an upside-down melting phenomenon.

Spain's 30-Year Vaccine Gap

Due to various factors including logistics and economics, Spain did not introduce the polio vaccine until 1963, long after other European nations. This delay led to the infamous "Paralyzed Generation" of the 1950s and early 60s.

Epic Scale
The Mahabharata, an ancient Indian epic that is considered a holy text by Hindus, is approximately ten times the length of "The Iliad" and "The Odyssey" combined and includes the Bhagavad Gita.

The Black-Eyed Children Phenomenon
Some people have reported encounters with children who have coal-black eyes and a spooky demeanor. These mysterious children supposedly ask to be let inside homes or vehicles, and the encounters are often described as intensely unsettling.

Zero's Late Arrival
The concept of zero was only formally introduced in the 7th century by Indian mathematician Brahmagupta, despite civilizations using other systems that needed a placeholder for nothing.

Two Ton Colossus
Colossus, created during World War II to break German codes, was the world's first programmable computer and used 2,500 vacuum tubes, occupying an entire room and weighing about two tons.

Quantum Teleportation
Quantum computers use a phenomenon analogous to teleportation known as quantum teleportation, but don't expect "Star Trek"-style teleporters. It's about transmitting quantum information between qubits using entanglement, crucial for quantum networking.

Data Breach Age
The largest data breach in history so far (Yahoo, 2013) affected 3 billion accounts, yet the full extent wasn't reported to the public until years later, raising ongoing conversations on notification practices.

Non-Algorithmic Speedup
Quantum computers have the potential to solve problems faster not by executing more instructions per second, but by transforming how those instructions are executed altogether in fundamentally new ways.

Phantom Touch
Some VR users experience a sensation known as phantom touch, where they feel touch in real life from interactions in a virtual environment, even though it's entirely simulated.

Aristotle's Animal Souls
Aristotle believed that animals possessed souls but differed from human souls. He proposed that while animals had sensitive souls responsible for movement and perception, humans had rational souls capable of reasoning.

The Ostrich Pillow (2012)
Designed for power naps, this pillow encases your head and hands, allowing you to nap on desks. It didn't go mainstream but found a niche following for its quirky design.

Chewbacca's Voices
The sounds for Chewbacca's character were made from a mix of several animals, including lions, bears, and walruses, carefully spliced together to create his unique voice.

Hobbiton is Real
The set constructed for "The Lord of the Rings" and "The Hobbit" movie trilogies, Hobbiton, remains a popular tourist attraction that you can visit near the town of Matamata.

Moken Sea Nomads
The Moken people, often referred to as "Sea Gypsies," live a nomadic lifestyle in the waters surrounding the Mergui Archipelago in Myanmar and Thailand. Known for their incredible swimming and diving abilities, they spend much of their lives on boats.

Australia's Western Null
The Nullarbor Plain in Australia, despite being one of the flattest parts of Earth's crust, was historically believed to hide great riches, leading to several exploratory expeditions that found only desolation.

Bankruptcy of Founder's Famous Invention

Despite inventing one of the most significant pieces of cinematic technology, Kodachrome film, Kodak's refusal to embrace digital photography advancements led to the company's bankruptcy in 2012.

The Brain Feels No Pain

While the brain processes pain from other parts of the body, it doesn't have pain receptors itself. This is why surgeons can perform certain types of brain surgery on awake patients without them feeling any pain in the brain itself.

Invention of Velcro

Velcro was invented by Swiss engineer George de Mestral in the 1940s. Inspired by how burrs stuck to his dog's fur, he developed the hook-and-loop fastener now used worldwide.

Annual Two-Sunlit Days

Antarctica experiences one long day and one long night annually, with 24-hour sunlight in summer and complete darkness in winter, due to its polar latitudes.

Milky Way

Camel's milk is a staple in arid regions and can be an essential part of food security strategies in these areas due to its ability to thrive in harsh conditions and its rich nutritional profile.

The Venus de Milo's Missing Arms

The Venus de Milo, a famous ancient Greek statue, was discovered without arms. The mystery of their original position and what they were doing has intrigued art historians for decades.

Dancing Plague of 1518

In the summer of 1518, a "dancing plague" struck Strasbourg (then part of the Holy Roman Empire), causing hundreds to dance compulsively for days without rest. The cause remains a mystery but highlights how psychological factors can influence public health crises.

Platypus Venom
The male platypus has venomous spurs on its hind legs, capable of delivering a painful sting to humans that can cause swelling, increased sensitivity to pain, and even long-lasting incapacitation.

SMS Turning 30
The first ever SMS text message was sent on December 3, 1992, in the UK. It read "Merry Christmas."

Vedic Recitation
Vedic hymns from the Rigveda, one of Hinduism's oldest texts, were traditionally passed down orally and have specific mnemonic techniques involving chanted patterns to ensure precise transmission over millennia.

Mangaian Sexual Practices
The Mangaia of Polynesia have traditionally placed a strong emphasis on sexual education and practices. Adolescents are taught extensively about sexual behaviors and are expected to be well-versed when they become adults, indicating a stark contrast to many Western attitudes toward sex education.

The Dingo Fence
To protect livestock from dingoes, Australia has one of the longest fences in the world, spanning over 5,600 kilometers (about 3,480 miles).

Jain Ahiṃsā
Jain monks and nuns practice such a high level of ahiṃsā (non-violence) that they sweep the ground before walking and wear face-covering cloths to avoid inhaling and harming tiny organisms.

Victor Hugo's Writing Routine
To prevent procrastination while writing "Les Misérables," Victor Hugo devised a peculiar strategy—he had his servant hide his clothes so he couldn't leave the house until he'd completed his writing goals for the day.

Giraffe Necks
While often cited as an example of natural selection, the long necks of giraffes aren't solely for reaching tall trees. They may have also evolved as a result of "necking," a combat behavior where males use their necks as weapons to compete for mates.

One-line factoids, bizarre truths and juicy chunks of wisdom

The Baby Cage (1930s)
A bizarre invention intended to provide city kids with fresh air, this wire cage was hung outside apartment windows. Safety concerns soon led to its disappearance.

Temple of Rats
Karni Mata Temple in Rajasthan is home to over 25,000 black rats, called "kabbas," which are revered and protected as they are believed to be the reincarnated relatives of the local goddess.

Invisible Art
Yves Klein, a French artist, created a series called "Zones of Immaterial Pictorial Sensibility" where he sold ownership receipts for invisible, non-existent works of art. Buyers had the option to trade back the receipt for a ritual burning and a trophy-gold exchange.

The Missing Island of Hy-Brasil
This mythical island was cartographically recorded as west of Ireland on various maps from the 14th to 19th centuries. However, its existence has never been confirmed, leading to rich folklore and tales of its supposed sightings and disappearances.

Samoa
It is considered illegal to forget your wife's birthday. Forgetting can potentially lead to serious domestic consequences!

AI and Gaming Victories
In 2019, an AI developed by OpenAI defeated a world champion team of human players in the video game "Dota 2". Before this, AI from DeepMind's AlphaGo program beat the world champion in Go, a game considered much more complex than chess.

The Phoenix Lights
On March 13, 1997, thousands of people across Arizona, Nevada, and Sonora, Mexico, reported seeing a massive, V-shaped craft with lights attached, silently gliding across the night sky. The event remains unexplained despite military flares offered as a possible explanation.

Bacteria Bonanza
About 90% of the cells in a human body are not human! They are actually mostly comprised of bacteria, many of which are necessary for good health.

The Legend of Melusine
In European folklore, Melusine is a female spirit of fresh water in sacred springs and rivers. She is often depicted as a serpent or fish from the waist down, much like a mermaid, but with two tails.

Ancient Societies and the Dogon People
The Dogon people of Mali have ancient tales that align eerily well with modern astronomy. They reportedly knew about the Sirius star system's companion star, which is invisible to the naked eye, long before it was discovered by telescopes.

Quantum Artificial Intelligence
Research is ongoing into using quantum computers to enhance artificial intelligence. Quantum enhancements could provide vast improvements in AI's ability to recognize patterns and learn, potentially revolutionizing fields like data analysis and machine learning.

The Eighth Continent Myth
During the Age of Exploration, European mapmakers often included a large 'Great Southern Land' or Terra Australis on maps based purely on speculation. This continent was only a hypothesis until the discovery of Australia and Antarctica.

Blue Banded Bees
Australia is home to the colorful blue-banded bee, which has a unique method of pollination called "buzz pollination," where the bee grabs onto a flower and vibrates powerfully enough to shake pollen out.

Pluralistic Ignorance
This is a situation where the majority of a group privately disagrees with a norm but goes along with it because they mistakenly believe everyone else in the group agrees with it. This can perpetuate societal norms that no one actually wants.

Chinese Automata

Ancient Chinese skill in metallurgy and engineering included the creation of automata — early robots powered by trickling water or weights, used to entertain and display craftsmanship.

Quantum Computing

Harnessing quantum principles, such as superposition and entanglement, quantum computers have the potential to solve certain problems far more efficiently than classical computers. This could revolutionize fields like cryptography, material science, and optimization.

Hybrid Combos

In "The Force Awakens," the sound of Rey's speeder was derived by blending a slowed-down recording of a busy Chevron gas station with a high-powered sports car engine.

Capgras Delusion

This disorder causes sufferers to believe that people close to them have been replaced by impostors, identical in appearance but not in authenticity.

Bacteria-Powered Batteries

Scientists have discovered that certain types of bacteria can generate electrical currents by eating organic material. This can lead to the development of microbial fuel cells that produce electricity from wastewater.

The Oak Island Money Pit

Located on Oak Island in Nova Scotia, Canada, the Money Pit is a site that has sparked treasure hunts for over 200 years. Supposedly containing a treasure buried by pirates or the Knights Templar, the pit is filled with traps and secret tunnels that have thwarted all excavation attempts.

The Missing Square Puzzle

This puzzling geometric illusion seems to suggest that rearranging the pieces of certain triangles creates a different area, but it's a trick relying on slightly differing slopes.

Alien Abduction Insurance

Believe it or not, some insurance companies offer policies that protect you against alien abductions. These plans cover cases of kidnapping by extraterrestrials, and while they might seem absurd, a few thousand people have bought them!

The Black Dahlia

In 1947, Elizabeth Short, nicknamed the "Black Dahlia," was found murdered and mutilated in Los Angeles. The case captured public fascination and remains one of the most famous unsolved murders in American history.

AI Mimicking Bird Calls

Researchers have developed AI systems that can simulate very accurate bird calls and even combine calls from different species to create unique new sounds. This helps in conservation efforts and the study of bioacoustics.

Lego's Resurgence Strategy

Once on the brink of bankruptcy, Lego turned its fortunes around by crowd-sourcing design ideas from fans through its Lego Ideas platform, which has led to creatively designed sets that are hugely popular.

One of the Largest Deserts

Despite being covered in ice, Antarctica is the world's largest desert. It receives very little precipitation, only about 2 inches each year.

Switching Typologies

Some languages have changed their basic word order dramatically over time. Japanese, for instance, is typically Subject-Object-Verb, while English mostly uses Subject-Verb-Object.

The Mary Celeste

In 1872, the ship Mary Celeste was found adrift with everything intact except for its crew, who had vanished without a trace. Theories abound, but the crew's fate remains a mystery.

Operation Migration

To teach endangered whooping cranes to migrate, pilots in ultralight aircraft have guided young birds along their migratory paths, leading them to wintering grounds.

Cat Sidhe's Soul Stealing

Scottish folklore talks about the Cat Sidhe, a fairy creature said to resemble a large black cat. Legend has it that the Cat Sidhe could steal the souls of the deceased before they were collected by the gods if a body was left unguarded.

The Dyatlov Pass Incident

In 1959, nine experienced hikers died under mysterious circumstances in the Ural Mountains. Their tent was torn open from the inside, and they fled inadequately dressed into the freezing wilderness. The cause remains unexplained.

Robot Bulls vs. AI Matadors

An AI program developed in the "RoboCup Soccer" competition is designed to control robot players in a football match. There are challenges focusing solely on AI-controlled robots to wrangle with realistic farming scenarios, like herding cows or interacting with fictional bull-like robots.

Giant Armadillos on Earth

Glyptodonts, which looked similar to giant armadillos and weighed up to two tons, roamed South America until about 10,000 years ago, coexisting with early humans.

Neotenic Salamanders

Axolotls retain juvenile traits throughout their adult life, a phenomenon known as neoteny. They are essentially "eternal larvae," able to reproduce without undergoing the usual metamorphosis seen in other amphibians.

Imaginary and Constructed Languages

Some languages are created entirely for fictional worlds, like Klingon in "Star Trek" or Dothraki in "Game of Thrones", complete with their own grammar and vocabulary.

Nebraska Man Hoax

In the early 20th century, a tooth initially thought to belong to an early human, dubbed "Nebraska Man," turned out to be from an extinct species of peccary, akin to a wild pig.

The Axeman of New Orleans

Active between 1918 and 1919, this mysterious figure hacked several people to death, mostly at night, and was never caught. In a bizarre twist, he claimed in a letter that he would spare anyone playing jazz music in their homes.

Jurassic Park's Dinosaur Roars

The terrifying roar of the T. rex in Steven Spielberg's "Jurassic Park" was a combination of various animal sounds, including a baby elephant, a lion, and an alligator, created by sound designer Gary Rydstrom.

Math and Astronomy

The Islamic Golden Age produced significant advancements in mathematics and astronomy, giving the world the algebra we know today and notable stars bearing Arabic names.

Dissociative Fugue

This rare disorder involves sudden, unexpected travel away from one's home, inability to recall one's past, leading to confusion about personal identity or adoption of a new identity, akin to a real-life amnesia movie plot.

Powerful Pinky

Your little finger, or pinky, contributes as much as 50% of your hand's strength.

Strange Incentives

In Japan, there's a unique environmental policy where companies receive carbon credits for initiatives such as reducing employee waistlines. It's part of their "Metabo Law," aimed not only at health but also at lowering healthcare costs and carbon footprints.

Sudden Wealth Syndrome

This is a term used to describe significant psychological distress that can occur when an individual suddenly comes into a large amount of money. The effects include paranoia, guilt, and confusion about personal relationships, highlighting the profound impact financial changes can have on one's social dynamics.

Tails and Balance

Both dogs and cats use their tails for balance, but cats are especially skilled at using them for climbing and walking along narrow spaces due to their agility and balance.

Time Dilation

Near a black hole, time slows down dramatically compared to distant observers. If you orbited a black hole for a short time and returned, you'd find more time had passed elsewhere.

Pangaea's Legacy

Around 300 million years ago, all the continents were joined in a supercontinent called Pangaea. This massive land formation completely reshaped the ancient world until it began breaking apart about 175 million years ago.

Traffic Lights Graffiti

In Tel Aviv, some pedestrian light signals feature playful and humorous designs, such as a figure sitting in a relaxed pose or holding balloons.

Invisible Forest on Your Skin

A square centimeter of human skin can hold up to two billion nanobacterial structures, which form a complex ecosystem on the skin surface.

Weird AI Poetry

There are AI models like GPT-3 that have been used to generate poetry, mixing language in unpredictable and sometimes profound ways. These AI poets sometimes produce content that feels surprisingly human in its depth and perspective.

Heart Health
Men are more likely to suffer heart attacks earlier in life than women, partly due to higher testosterone levels, which can increase the risk of cardiovascular events.

The Trans-Siberian Railway
Stretching over 9,289 kilometers (5,772 miles), it's the longest railway line in the world, connecting Moscow with Vladivostok. A non-stop journey takes about a week!

The Hawthorne Effect
This term originated from a study conducted at the Hawthorne Works factory, where researchers found that workers increased their productivity simply because they knew they were being observed, not necessarily because of any specific change in work environment.

Pica
This eating disorder involves the persistent ingestion of non-nutritive substances, such as dirt, clay, or chalk, particularly surprising because it can occur in people of all ages.

The Green Children of Woolpit
In 12th-century England, two children with green skin reportedly appeared in the village of Woolpit. Although they eventually lost their green hue, their origins were never fully explained, sparking tales of otherworldly visits.

Enduring Eco-Villages
The French eco-village, "Les Jardins de l'Écureuil," pays families to compost at home, collecting the organic waste weekly which helps meet a collective zero waste goal.

The Dying Art of Yodeling
While known globally for yodeling, Switzerland is actually struggling to keep this tradition alive. Efforts are underway to revive interest in this unique art form.

Midnight Sun Golfing

In northern Norway, you can play a full round of golf in the middle of the night during the summer months thanks to the midnight sun. It's a surreal experience to tee off at 2 AM in broad daylight!

Canada (Petrolia, Ontario)

It's against the law to "yell, shout, hoot, whittle or sing" in public places. This rule is meant to curb excessive noise.

Food Loss Paradox

While about one-third of food produced is wasted globally each year, just one-fourth of that lost food could feed all the world's hungry people, illustrating both a logistical and ethical dilemma in food security.

Bear Classrooms in Russia

In some parts of Russia, students can take classes that train them to interact and care for bears—a traditional skill in regions where bear dancing remains a cultural practice.

Mistaken Messenger

In the infamous case of O.J. Simpson, a glove left at the crime scene was a pivotal piece of evidence, showcasing how an ordinary object can transform into a courtroom sensation.

Flying Spaghetti Monster

The Church of the Flying Spaghetti Monster, or Pastafarianism, is a satirical religion that critiques creationism and intelligent design, featuring a deity made of spaghetti and meatballs.

Amarnath Cave Ice Lingam

The Amarnath Cave in India features a naturally forming ice lingam, considered a representation of Lord Shiva, which waxes and wanes with the phases of the moon, attracting thousands of pilgrims annually.

Color Change

Gold, when broken down into nanoparticles, does not exhibit its characteristic color. Instead, it appears red or purple depending on the size of the particles, which is due to quantum effects influencing its optical properties.

Spider Rain

In some parts of Australia, there's a phenomenon known as "spider rain," where millions of small spiders blanket the land with webs that look like eerie, silky sheets. This occurs when spiders use their webs to catch the wind and disperse, a process called "ballooning."

Valiant Thor

A man claiming to be an alien visitor named Valiant Thor allegedly met with high-level U.S. officials in the late 1950s. According to conspiracy theorists, he came from Venus to offer aid—which the government purportedly declined.

Global Movement for Free Education

In Norway, like other Nordic countries, higher education is free, including for international students, which contrasts starkly with the high tuition fees in other parts of the world like the United States.

Earliest Witches as Healers

In ancient Mesopotamia, witchcraft was often synonymous with healing. Tablets record incantations and rituals designed to heal people from illnesses, thought to be inflicted by vengeful spirits.

Cotard's Syndrome

Individuals with Cotard's Syndrome, or "walking corpse syndrome," believe they are dead, do not exist, or have lost their organs or blood.

Pandas' Faux Pas

During China's panda breeding efforts, some female pandas are shown "panda pornography," videos of other pandas mating, to stimulate their mating instincts.

Authors Over Time

The authors of the Bible span a period of 1,500 years, from Moses (traditional author of the first five books) to John the Apostle in the late 1st century AD.

The Mona Lisa's Theft

The Mona Lisa, arguably the world's most famous painting, was stolen from the Louvre in 1911. The thief, an Italian named Vincenzo Peruggia, believed it should be returned to Italy. It was recovered two years later and the theft incident ironically elevated its fame.

The Longest Traffic Jam

The longest traffic jam in history occurred in China in 2010. It stretched over 62 miles and lasted for 12 days on the Beijing-Tibet Expressway.

Meticulous Kubrick

For "The Shining," Stanley Kubrick shot approximately 1.3 million feet of film, which is over 237 hours of footage, due to his desire for perfection. The film's famous "Here's Johnny!" scene alone required 60 doors.

The Henrietta Lacks Case

The HeLa cells, taken without consent from Henrietta Lacks in 1951, have been used in countless medical breakthroughs, including the polio vaccine, without her knowledge or compensation to her family for many years, sparking major ethical debates about patient rights and consent.

Virtual Depression Therapy

Research has shown that embodying a character in VR can help treat depression. By controlling a virtual character, patients can engage in perspective-switching exercises that help them develop self-compassion and cope with their emotions better.

Inverted Grids

In San Antonio, Texas, streets are intentionally planned using a misaligned grid system to deter potential criminal behaviors, enhancing safety by confusing malicious activity seekers.

Solar Paint

Scientists have been developing a "solar paint" that can generate hydrogen gas by splitting water vapor using sunlight, potentially allowing buildings to produce their own energy.

The Radio-Quiet Zone of Vostochny

In an effort to minimize interference with astronomical observations, some regions in Russia, like Vostochny Cosmodrome, are radio-quiet, restricting electromagnetic emissions.

Miraculous Caterpillars

Legend has it that in the 17th century, the followers of Father John Paul Miki, a Japanese saint, witnessed caterpillars transform into beautiful butterflies upon touching his relic, signifying his sainthood.

Venomous Mammals

Some mammals, like the male platypus, produce venom. While venom is more common in reptiles, insects, and marine organisms, a few mammals have retained or evolved this trait independently.

Firework Ban in Bhutan

Bhutan banned the production, sale, and use of fireworks in 2006 to prevent noise pollution and to reflect the country's commitment to maintaining peace and tranquility.

Turing Test

A fun aspect of Philosophy of Mind argues that if a computer can convince a human that it is also human, then it's intelligent. However, people wonder amusingly if computers should then pay taxes!

Martian Bowling Alley

There's a persistent rumor that NASA's Opportunity rover found shapes resembling bowling pins on Mars — sparking imagined stories of Martian games.

Emoji Bones

Humans and giraffes have the same number of neck vertebrae—seven. It's just that a giraffe's are much longer!

The Polar Express Face Controversy

"The Polar Express" was among the first films to utilize performance capture technology. Despite technical advancements, audiences found the human characters unsettling due to their uncanny resemblance to wax figures.

One-line factoids, bizarre truths and juicy chunks of wisdom

The Fishwalker (1940s)
This peculiar device allowed fish to be carried in a small amount of water, like a pet on a leash. Due to impracticality, it never reached an aquarist audience.

Gold's Solubility
Gold does not dissolve in nitric acid, which dissolves most other metals, but it does dissolve in aqua regia, a mixture of nitric and hydrochloric acid, which is how alchemists distinguished it from many other materials.

Pinterest's Original Purpose
Pinterest, launched in 2010, was initially conceived as an app to help people plan their weddings.

Schumann's Finger Injury
Composer Robert Schumann aspired to be a virtuoso pianist, but a self-inflicted hand injury from using a homemade device to strengthen his fingers ended his piano-playing dreams.

Mango Auctions
The first tray of mangoes of the season is annually auctioned off for charity in Australia, often reaching tens of thousands of dollars, showing the fruit's beloved status.

Insect Clues
Forensic entomology uses insect activity to estimate time of death. Blowflies can arrive on a corpse within minutes of death, and their life cycle stages give crucial timing clues.

Turquoise Hydrogen
Turquoise hydrogen is produced via methane pyrolysis, generating solid carbon instead of CO_2 as a byproduct, posing an interesting low-emission alternative to conventional hydrogen production.

Plastic Bag Bans Go Way Back
Denmark was the first country in the world to implement a law restricting the use of plastic bags back in 1993. They introduced a tax that encouraged people to use reusable bags instead.

Reviving Extinct Species
Genetic engineering, especially through CRISPR (clustered regularly interspaced short palindromic repeats), is being explored as a means to potentially bring back extinct species such as the woolly mammoth. Researchers aim to splice mammoth genes into the DNA of Asian elephants.

Australia (Victoria)
It is illegal to change a light bulb unless you are a licensed electrician. This law was introduced for safety reasons.

Rice and Water
Paddy rice fields use about 30% of the world's freshwater resources, highlighting a critical intersection of agriculture and water security challenges.

Longest Verse
The longest verse in the Bible is Esther 8:9. It has 90 words in the original Hebrew.

Swedish Blood Sausage Ice Cream
In Sweden, you can find "blodpudding" (blood sausage) as an ice cream flavor, often served as a culinary challenge for adventurous eaters.

Survival of the Unemployed Economy
In some countries with very high unemployment rates, informal economies or black markets have sprung up to levels comparable in size to legitimate economies, showing how adaptive economic systems can be.

Space Gold Rush
Asteroids like 16 Psyche are rich in valuable minerals. This particular asteroid is believed to be mostly made of metal, potentially worth quintillions of dollars, sparking dreams of future interstellar mining.

The Circleville Letters
In the 1970s and 80s, a small Ohio town was terrorized by an anonymous sender of menacing letters. One suspect was arrested but the letters continued to arrive even after his imprisonment, and the mystery was never solved.

Lake Retba
Often referred to as "Lac Rose," this pink-colored lake in Senegal gets its unusual hue from the Dunaliella salina algae, which produce a red pigment to help them absorb sunlight.

World's Largest Gathering
The Kumbh Mela festival, held every 12 years, is the largest religious gathering in the world. In 2013, it attracted over 30 million people in a single day.

Unusual Banknote Features
The Swiss issued a banknote focused on the scientific exploits and achievements unique to the country; their 9th series of banknotes even won awards for their innovative design and security features.

The Zodiac Killer's Cryptograms
The infamous Zodiac Killer, active in the late 1960s in California, sent taunting letters with cryptograms to newspapers. Most have been decoded, but one remains unsolved, hiding potentially crucial information about his identity.

Nano-Hearing Aids
Researchers are using nanotechnology to develop advanced hearing aids with even smaller, more powerful components, potentially offering better sound quality and feedback reduction.

No Official Head of State
Switzerland operates without a single head of state. Instead, it has a Federal Council consisting of seven members who share executive power equally, with one of them serving as president for just one year.

Zombie Satellites
There are satellites, often called "zombie satellites," that lose communication with Earth but continue orbiting the planet. Occasionally, they make unexpected contact years later, like the resurrected IMAGE satellite.

Kumbh Mela Phenomenon
The Kumbh Mela, a massive pilgrimage gathering, is recognized as the world's largest human congregation. In 2013, over 30 million people gathered in a single day.

Fake Snow In "The Wizard of Oz"
The snow used in the poppy field scene of "The Wizard of Oz" was made from asbestos, a health hazard unrecognized at the time.

Wind Turbine Deathmatch
Some wind turbines are being designed to combat ice buildup on their blades. They use electromagnetic pulses or even drone-deployed heating techniques to eliminate ice, preventing damage and loss of efficiency.

Sleeping with the Ghosts
Sweden offers an extraordinary experience with the "Utter Inn," an underwater accommodation where you can sleep 3 meters below the surface of Lake Mälaren and possibly dream above ghostly surges from centuries past.

The Hard Problem of Consciousness
Coined by David Chalmers, this problem questions why and how physical processes in our brains give rise to subjective experience—a query so elusive it sounds more like a riddle than a solvable problem.

The Lost City of Z
The Amazon was once home to complex civilizations with cities that rivaled those of Europe, but many were abandoned and overtaken by the jungle. The exploration of these cities inspired tales like the mythical "El Dorado."

Underwater Black Smokers
In hydrothermal vent fields, chimney-like structures called black smokers expel superheated water rich in minerals. These extreme environments support unique ecosystems reliant on chemosynthesis rather than photosynthesis.

Mentawai's Body Art

The Mentawai people of Siberut Island in Indonesia are famous for their extensive body art, including tattoos and teeth sharpening. Their intricate tattoos depict spiritual significances tied to nature and ancestry.

The Wow! Signal

In 1977, astronomer Jerry R. Ehman detected a strong narrowband radio signal from outer space with the Big Ear radio telescope. Dubbed the "Wow! Signal," its origins have never been identified, leaving it a tantalizing potential extraterrestrial transmission.

The Vanished Aral Sea

Once the fourth-largest inland lake in the world, the Aral Sea has dramatically shrunk since the 1960s due to the diversion of the rivers that fed it for irrigation projects, rendering much of its original area a desert today.

St. Valentine

There are actually several Christian martyrs named Valentine. The most famous one, St. Valentine, is associated with love and is believed to have secretly performed weddings for soldiers forbidden to marry, which led to his martyrdom.

Quantum Dots

These are nanoscale semiconductor particles with optical and electronic properties that change based on their size and are being explored for use in displays, solar cells, and biological imaging.

Weather Modification Treaties

In 1978, the United Nations enacted the Environmental Modification Convention, which prohibits the military or other hostile use of environmental modification techniques. This means countries agreed not to use weather modification as a means of warfare.

Lip Prints

Just like fingerprints, lip prints are unique to every individual. This means they can sometimes be used as evidence, a practice known as cheiloscopy.

Truman Show Delusion
Named after the movie, some people believe they are the unwitting stars of a reality-television show, with everyone in their life playing a role.

Shortest Verse
The shortest verse in the Bible is John 11:35, "Jesus wept," which is only two words long.

D-Wave's Approach
D-Wave Systems is a company that focuses on a type of quantum computing called quantum annealing, which is designed to solve optimization problems quickly. Their systems already have over 5000 qubits, but the debate is ongoing about whether this approach achieves the same expected quantum computational benefits as gate-model quantum computers.

The Dynasphere (1930)
A monowheel vehicle shaped like a giant hoop, it lacked practicality and stability, confining it to the history books instead of highways.

E.T. Cameo
In "The Phantom Menace," during a Galactic Senate scene, you can spot members of E.T.'s species among the senate pods, a nod to Spielberg and Lucas's friendship.

Baobab Trees
Known as the "Tree of Life," some larger baobabs can store more than 31,700 gallons of water to endure drought conditions and can live for over a thousand years.

Africa's Triple Junction
In the Afar region of Ethiopia lies the Afar Triple Junction, a geological wonder where three tectonic plates intersect. This is one of the only places on Earth where you can observe a rift developing on land.

Heavy Water
Deuterium oxide, or "heavy water," is used in nuclear reactors and looks just like regular water, but it's about 10% heavier due to the presence of deuterium, an isotope of hydrogen.

Unicorn of the Sea
Narwhals are known for their long, spiral tusks, which can grow up to 10 feet. This tusk is actually an evolved elongated tooth, and the evolutionary reasons behind it possibly involve social or sexual signals.

Uterus Transplants
Uterus transplants have challenged existing views on fertility and the capability of transgender women or non-uterus-bearing individuals to potentially carry a pregnancy, sparking debates about the limits of reproductive technology.

Black Hole Sun
Some black holes consume matter so fiercely that they can shine brighter than all the stars in their galaxy, thanks to the energy released by infalling matter.

AI Writing "Harry Potter" Fan Fiction
A recurrent neural network was trained on all seven "Harry Potter" books and then tasked with generating its own version of a new chapter. The resulting text was nonsensical but amusing, showcasing AI's ability to mimic writing styles.

Worms for Justice
In the 1850 murder case of George Bodle, maggots found on the victim's liver helped forensic pioneer William Little determine the time of death, influencing the court's decision.

Language-Mix AI
AI models have been developed that can translate languages they weren't explicitly trained on due to their understanding of linguistic structures, which sometimes even includes languages never inputted into their system.

Whip-Smart Wrinkles
The human brain releases the same happiness-inducing neurotransmitter, dopamine, during orgasm as it does during a satisfying meal or drug high, emphasizing the complex reward system associated with sexual activity.

The Edible Energy Grass

Miscanthus, an innovative biofuel crop, can grow up to 13 feet in a season, absorbs large amounts of CO2, and is being researched as a potent source of bioenergy.

Finland's No Homework Policy

Finland is renowned for its unconventional approach to education by giving little to no homework. Despite this, Finnish students perform exceptionally well in international assessments, suggesting that more homework isn't necessarily the key to learning.

Giant Stones as Currency

In the Micronesian island of Yap, enormous stone disks known as Rai stones have been used as currency. Some are as large as 12 feet in diameter! The value is not in the stone itself but in its history and ownership.

Banana Extinction Prevention

Banana crops worldwide are threatened by a fungus called Panama disease. Genetic engineering aims to create disease-resistant banana varieties to prevent the fruit from going extinct.

Body Scarification in Africa

In several African cultures, scarification is used as a form of social identification and as a marker of beauty, adulthood, or courage. Elaborate scars are carefully created on the skin, often associated with tribal, spiritual, or personal meaning.

Van Gogh's Ear Incident

In 1888, Vincent van Gogh famously cut off part of his ear after a heated argument with fellow artist Paul Gauguin. The exact motivations remain unclear, leading to much speculation and myth-making over the years.

The Åland Island Holiday Mystery

This Finnish archipelago celebrates its own unique holiday called Åland Day on June 9th, which is mainly marked by general island pride and a day off work, despite its somewhat mysterious origins.

One-line factoids, bizarre truths and juicy chunks of wisdom

Sharks Detect Electricity

Sharks have special sensors known as ampullae of Lorenzini, which enable them to detect the electrical fields produced by living organisms, helping them hunt even when they can't see their prey.

World's First Documented Laws

The Code of Hammurabi, inscribed on a stone stele in Babylon, predates many modern law codes and was incredibly detailed, governing aspects of daily life and justice.

The Kelly-Hopkinsville Encounter

In 1955, a family in Kentucky claimed they spent a night fighting off small, goblin-like creatures that attacked their farmhouse. The event involved multiple witnesses and led to an extensive police investigation, but no evidence was found.

Weight limit infringement

It's illegal to be overweight! The "Metabo Law" in Japan sets specific waistline limits for men (85 cm) and women (90 cm).

Cyberostracism

This term refers to being ignored or excluded in online social interactions, which can have effects on individuals that are just as severe as face-to-face exclusion, demonstrating the significant impact of digital environments on our social well-being.

Chicken from Hell

An enormous dinosaur, Anzu wyliei, was nicknamed the "Chicken from Hell" due to its bird-like appearance and large size. This dinosaur stood roughly seven feet tall and had a beak, feathers, and claws.

Ancient Greek Vending Machines

Invented by Hero of Alexandria, the earliest known vending machine dispensed holy water. Users placed a coin in the machine, which would trigger a lever to release a measured amount of liquid.

Jataka Tales

In Buddhist literature, the Jataka tales recount over 500 stories of the Buddha's previous lives, illustrating moral lessons and the concept of reincarnation.

Hot Ice

Sodium acetate, used in hand warmers, can produce "hot ice." When a super-saturated solution of sodium acetate is disturbed, it crystallizes rapidly, releasing heat in the process.

Panpsychism

This theory suggests that consciousness is a fundamental and ubiquitous aspect of the universe, with even elementary particles having some level of consciousness. It takes the phrase "everything has a mind" to a whole new level.

Pharrell Williams' Timeless Look

Despite being born in 1973, Pharrell Williams seems to never age, leading fans to joke that he's a vampire.

The Hamsa Hand

Used as a protective symbol in Judaism, the hamsa (or "Hand of Miriam") is believed to ward off the evil eye and bring good fortune.

Biofluorescent Plants

Researchers have edited the genes of plants to make them biofluorescent, which could lead to future glowing trees that could replace street lights, reducing energy consumption.

Tightly Packed Tokyo

Tokyo Yamanote Line is famous for its bullet trains traveling on average one minute apart at peak times, catering to over one million passengers daily on just this loop line alone!

Vulture Restaurants

Facilities called "vulture restaurants" have been set up in South Africa, providing safe carcasses free of poisons for the dwindling vulture populations.

Color Perception

Women generally have more color receptors in their eyes, which can make them better at distinguishing subtle color differences than men. This is why men might argue about whether a color is teal or turquoise!

One-line factoids, bizarre truths and juicy chunks of wisdom

Ed Wood's Continuity Blunders
The 1959 film "Plan 9 from Outer Space", directed by Ed Wood, is famous for its continuity blunders: day turns to night and back again in mere seconds due to a lack of budget and planning.

Thaipusam Festival in Malaysia
Celebrated mostly by the Tamil community, during Thaipusam, some devotees pierce their bodies with hooks and skewers as acts of devotion and penance, walking long distances to reach temples during this intense festival.

The Little Death
In French, orgasm is referred to as "la petite mort" or "the little death," highlighting the brief loss of consciousness and the euphoric state some experience at climax.

The Indian Railways Mail Network
Indian Railways has its own postal service with dedicated trains to carry mail across the country, managing the world's largest mail circulatory system.

Placebo Surgeries
Some clinical trials use sham surgeries, where patients believe they are receiving a surgical procedure when they are not, to test the efficacy of operations - raising ethical questions about consent and potential harm to participants.

Mirror Neurons
These are a type of brain cell that fires both when an individual performs an action and when they observe someone else performing the same action. They are believed to play a role in empathy and learning through imitation.

St. Petersburg's White Nights
Between May and July, the city experiences near-endless daylight, known as "White Nights," due to its high latitude. The phenomenon draws many to enjoy its cultural festivals.

Multiple Realizability

This idea suggests that mental states can be realized in many different physical systems. This leads to bizarre questions like whether an alien or computer could experience pain when they exhibit pain-like behavior.

Fruit Naming

Anakin Skywalker's character in early drafts of "Star Wars: Episode I — The Phantom Menace" was reportedly named "Anakin Starkiller," a name chosen because it reminded Lucas of familiar, down-to-earth fruit—"starkillers."

Lunar Lawns

It's illegal to own a piece of the Moon under the Outer Space Treaty. Nonetheless, thousands of people have "deeds" to lunar property, thanks to enterprising salesmen, though such claims hold no legal weight.

The Bobo Doll Experiment

Conducted by Albert Bandura in the 1960s, this study demonstrated that children could learn aggression through observation, challenging existing notions that aggression is only biologically determined.

Angelina Jolie's Lips Inspired Doll

The famous Bratz dolls were initially inspired by Angelina Jolie's distinctive lips, contributing to their iconic design.

Helium's Escape Act

Earth's helium reserves are slowly escaping into space. Because helium is so light, it can reach escape velocity and drift off into the void, never to return.

Jack the Ripper

This unidentified serial killer terrorized London in 1888, brutally murdering several women in and around the Whitechapel district. The case is still open, and many suspect theories exist.

Electric Fish

Some fish, such as the electric eel, have evolved the ability to generate electric fields. These adaptations are used for navigation, communication, and hunting in murky waters.

One-line factoids, bizarre truths and juicy chunks of wisdom

Bone Farming

The "body farm" at the University of Tennessee studies decomposition in various conditions to simulate crime scene scenarios, assisting forensic research and training.

Peloton's Subscription Success

Peloton, a company renowned for its innovative exercise equipment, makes more money from its monthly subscription services than from the equipment itself, highlighting a shift towards service economies over product sales.

Sinking Cathedral

In Brittany, France, there is a legend about a sunken city called Ys, which is tied to Christianity through the tale of St. Winwaloe, who warned the people about their wickedness, leading to the city's supposed downfall.

Colossal Longest Word

The longest word may vary by language, but in English, one of the longest coined words is the chemical name for the protein "titin", which is 189,819 letters long when spelled out fully.

Zombie Argument

Some philosophers propose the possibility of "philosophical zombies," beings identical to humans in every way except they lack conscious experience. This is used in debates about consciousness and the mind-body problem.

Tallest Brick Minaret

Qutub Minar in Delhi, standing 72.5 meters high, is the world's tallest brick minaret. Built in the 12th century, it is a UNESCO World Heritage Site and a testament to Indo-Islamic architecture.

Basquiat's Mysterious Signature

Jean-Michel Basquiat often used a recurring motif of a crown in his artworks. It was his signature symbol, signifying his self-identification with kingship, authority, and a mark of excellence.

Forests of Solar Panels

China is leading in renewable energy and has some of the largest solar farms, including a solar plant shaped like a panda!

The Immortal Beings
Hindu mythology includes several chiranjeevis, or immortals, who are believed to have existed since the ancient times and continue to live today, such as Ashwatthama, King Mahabali, and Hanuman.

Animal Immunization
The use of genetic modification in animals to produce pharmaceutical proteins, like insulin in "pharming," raises dilemmas regarding animal rights and the extent of human intervention in nature.

The Wettest Place on Earth
Mawsynram, a village in the state of Meghalaya, holds the record for the highest average annual rainfall. It's one of the wettest places on the planet, receiving around 467 inches of rain a year.

Buddhist Prayer Flags
In Tibetan Buddhism, colorful prayer flags are believed to spread blessings and prayers with the wind, symbolizing concepts like peace, compassion, and wisdom.

Zombie Phone Armies
A massive botnet of compromised mobile devices, known as "zombies," can be used without the owners' knowledge to launch coordinated attacks or run malicious activities.

Aztec "Flower Wars"
The Aztecs engaged in "flower wars," ritual combat intended not to expand territory but to capture prisoners for sacrificial purposes. Victors gained prestige but were expected to capture, not kill, their opponents.

DNA Origami
Researchers are able to fold DNA strands into nanoscale structures and shapes, such as smiley faces, boxes, and even miniature castles, through a process known as DNA origami.

YouTube's Humble Start
The first-ever video uploaded to YouTube by co-founder Jawed Karim on April 23, 2005, is titled "Me at the zoo" and features Karim at the San Diego Zoo.

One-line factoids, bizarre truths and juicy chunks of wisdom

The EgyptianPharaohs' Tradition
Ancient Egyptian pharaohs would ritually masturbate into the Nile as a fertility ritual to ensure a rich and prosperous harvest.

Octopus Parenting
The male Argonaut octopus gets rid of its mating arm after copulation. This specialized arm can crawl to a female on its own to provide sperm, and the male grows a new one later.

The Skin's Weight
Your skin is the largest and heaviest organ of your body, with an average adult's skin weighing around 8-10 pounds.

James Joyce's Elaborate Eye Patch
The famous Irish author James Joyce suffered from numerous eye problems and frequently needed surgery. To protect his sensitive eyes, he often wore an eye patch. What's bizarre is that he reportedly had a collection of colorful and decorative eye patches.

Parachuting Beavers
In a 1950s Idaho conservation effort, beavers were relocated to more suitable habitats by air-dropping them in specially designed parachuted crates. Surprisingly, it worked!

Luke's Original Fate
Early drafts for "Return of the Jedi" had Luke becoming the new Vader by putting on his mask, signaling his turn to the dark side before the final plot was decided.

AI in Fashion Design
AI is being used to create new fashion designs, blending different styles, trends, and seasons. For example, an Amazon AI patent proposes a system that designs clothing based on machine learning models and fashion databases.

The Anti-Bandit Bag (1960s)
Designed with a mechanism to spill contents when thieves snatched it, the bag's reliability issues and potential mess kept it from wide adoption.

Pauli Exclusion Principle

No two fermions, such as electrons, can occupy the same quantum state simultaneously within a quantum system. This principle is fundamental to the structure of atoms and the creation of the periodic table of elements.

Fireworks and Weather

Some firework events have been postponed because fireworks can sometimes intensify fog by condensing in the air moisture, significantly reducing visibility.

Galactic Cannibalism

It's believed that larger galaxies grow by "eating" smaller galaxies and their black holes, merging to create even more massive central black holes.

Silent Classrooms in India

In some innovative Indian schools, students are encouraged to learn in silence through specialized materials that promote self-directed study and reflection, aligning with the principles of certain meditative practices.

Syncretism in Voodoo

Voodoo is a syncretic religion combining elements of West African traditions, Catholicism, and indigenous beliefs, leading to unique practices like spirit possession and elaborate rituals.

Tsodilo Hills Art

The Tsodilo Hills in Botswana contain one of the world's highest concentrations of rock art—over 4,500 paintings, some of which date back tens of thousands of years, hinting at rich prehistoric human activity.

Satanic Temple's Advocacy

Despite the name, the Satanic Temple doesn't worship Satan. Instead, it uses symbolism to advocate for secularism, religious freedom, and social justice, often through provocative legal and cultural actions.

Night Vision

Cats can see in near-total darkness thanks to a structure called the tapetum lucidum, which reflects light through the retina. Dogs also have this feature, but cats are better adapted for night vision.

Iceland's No Last Name System
Icelandic citizens' last names are often derived from their father's (or sometimes mother's) first name, with the suffix -son or -dóttir, meaning son or daughter, making family ancestry quite unique.

World's Most Liked Instagram Post
As of 2019, an egg became the most-liked photo on Instagram, surpassing 56 million likes. The account started a social experiment to beat the previous record held by Kylie Jenner.

Tasmanian Devil Facial Tumor
Tasmanian devils are plagued by a contagious cancer. Conservationists employ quarantine and breeding programs to prevent population extinction.

Olmec Colossal Heads
The Olmecs, an ancient civilization in present-day Mexico, created giant stone heads up to 10 feet tall and 20 tons in weight. How they transported these massive sculptures remains a mystery.

Flying Saint
St. Joseph of Copertino (1603–1663) was known for reportedly levitating during prayer or in religious ecstasy. Due to these supernatural occurrences, he became the patron saint of air travelers and astronauts.

Vegetarian Prophet
Some historical texts suggest that the Prophet Muhammad followed and advocated a semi-vegetarian diet, emphasizing moderation and ethical treatment of animals.

The First Virus
The first computer virus, known as the "Creeper," was created in 1971. It was a harmless experimental program that spread by replicating itself, and its creator also made a program called "Reaper" to remove it.

Buddhist Self-Mummification
The Sokushinbutsu were Buddhist monks in Japan who attempted to mummify themselves while alive through a strict diet, meditation, and burial, seen as an ultimate act of enlightenment.

Blind Cavefish
Some species of cave-dwelling fish, like the Mexican tetra, have evolved to lose their eyesight completely. Living in complete darkness, these fish don't need vision and have repurposed the energy and biological resources towards other senses.

Direction Navigation
Men often rely on directional and distance cues for navigation, while women are more likely to use landmarks and locations, which can affect how each gender approaches wayfinding tasks.

Deep Blue Defeats a Chess Master
IBM's Deep Blue became the first computer to defeat a reigning world chess champion, Garry Kasparov, in a full match in 1997. Kasparov won the first match in 1996, sparking intrigue and debates over AI in chess.

Immune System
Women's immune systems are often more robust than men's, providing better responses to infections and vaccines but also making them more susceptible to autoimmune diseases.

Soap Bubbles Freeze
At temperatures below −15°C (5°F), soap bubbles can freeze and turn into a crystal ball in midair before they hit the ground.

The Disappearance of D.B. Cooper
In 1971, a man known as D.B. Cooper hijacked a plane, demanded a ransom of $200,000, jumped out with a parachute, and was never found. Despite extensive investigations, his identity and whereabouts remain unknown.

The Hum
In certain locations around the world, residents report hearing a persistent low-frequency hum with no identifiable source. The phenomenon remains a mystery, and while possible explanations involve industrial equipment or geological activities, some attribute it to extraterrestrial origins.

Vinegar Light at Havdalah
While the Havdalah ceremony typically involves wine, spices, and a candle, some communities have used vinegar-soaked wicks to ignite the light, symbolizing a bright beginning to the forthcoming week.

Komodo Dragon Ancestors
The ancestors of modern Komodo dragons once inhabited Australia and were much larger. Megalania, which reached lengths of over 23 feet, was the largest known terrestrial lizard to have ever existed.

IoT Threats
In 2017, a casino in North America was hacked through an internet-connected fish tank thermometer, highlighting the unusual vulnerabilities of Internet of Things (IoT) devices.

Vine's Short Life
Vine, the 6-second video platform, launched in 2013 and amassed over 200 million active users by 2016 but was abruptly shut down by Twitter, which acquired it, due largely to competition and monetization issues.

Sound Waves from a Black Hole
In 2003, scientists discovered sound waves coming from a supermassive black hole in the Perseus cluster, pitched at 57 octaves below middle C.

Virtual Reality's Long History
Virtual reality equipment dates back to the 1960s, with the Sensorama, a multi-sensory machine. However, it didn't gain significant traction until technology advances in the 21st century, demonstrating how long it can take for some innovations to become mainstream.

The Zodiac Killer
Active in the late 1960s and early 1970s in Northern California, the Zodiac Killer teasingly communicated with police through cryptic letters. Despite several suspects, the killer's identity has never been definitively proven.

Yanomami Belief in Reincarnation
The Yanomami tribe in the Amazon rainforest believe in endocannibalism, where they consume the ashes of their deceased relatives through a special banana soup. They believe this act helps the spirit of the deceased to find peace and be reincarnated.

Boanthropy

This rare delusion causes an individual to believe and behave as if they are a cow or an ox, including grazing habits.

Perfect Numbers and Their Mystical Connections

Perfect numbers, like 6 and 28, are equal to the sum of their proper divisors. In ancient times, they were thought to have mystical properties.

Orson Welles Almost Voiced Darth Vader

Instead of James Earl Jones, George Lucas initially considered Orson Welles for the voice of Darth Vader. He thought Welles's voice would be too recognizable.

Greenland's Misleading Name

Erik the Red named Greenland effectively as a marketing strategy to attract settlers. Historically, it was never as green and fertile as its name suggests, though during the Medieval Warm Period, Norse settlers did farm there for a time.

Silent Symphony

Your body plays a symphony of noise 24/7, from your heartbeat to the gurgling of your stomach, yet you usually only notice them when they stop!

Redundant Stomachs

Ruminants like cows and giraffes have a highly specialized digestive system with multiple stomachs to maximize the efficiency of digesting tough plant material, an adaptation that allows access to a steady food source.

Hacker Prank War

In 1999, NASA's website was hacked by a group called "Phantom Lord" who left a message: "The traffic comets are entering your atmosphere." They were part of a hacking "prank war" with other groups.

Whale Calling in the Philippines

The Balyanos or whale callers of Lamon Bay perform rituals using percussion with traditional instruments to call to passing whales. This ritual has been passed down generations, though its effectiveness is more symbolic than practical.

One-line factoids, bizarre truths and juicy chunks of wisdom

Bone Hard Facts
Humans are born with 300 bones, many of which fuse together over time, leaving adults with 206 bones.

Mere Exposure Effect
Repeated exposure to certain people or objects tends to increase our preference for them. This principle explains why you might start to enjoy a song after hearing it on the radio multiple times, or why you might feel an inexplicable fondness for coworkers you see regularly.

Kalash Valley's Unique Religion
The Kalash people in Pakistan have a religion distinct from both Islam and Hinduism, with Indo-European roots and worship of nature and ancestral spirits. They are known for their vibrant festivals and unique cultural practices.

The Unlikely Decline of Guinea Worm Disease
Guinea worm disease has seen a 99.99% drop in cases in the last 30 years, going from an estimated 3.5 million cases in 1986 to only 13 cases reported in 2022, showcasing one of the most successful eradication campaigns in public health history.

Urban Agriculture
During World War II, victory gardens, also known as war gardens, provided nearly 40% of all the vegetables consumed in the U.S., showing the power of localized food production in times of crisis.

MOOCs Emergence
The rise of Massive Open Online Courses (MOOCs) has revolutionized education access. The bizarre part is how they went from virtually nonexistent to enrolling hundreds of thousands of students worldwide in just a few years.

The Broken Windows Theory
This theory suggests that visible signs of disorder and neglect, such as broken windows, can encourage further crime and anti-social behavior. A single broken window can allegedly lead to more windows being broken, gradually causing entire communities to enter a state of disrepair and lawlessness.

Naked Eye Craftsmanship

The International Space Station is the largest human-made object in space and can be seen with the naked eye from Earth, appearing as a bright moving point across the night sky.

Ocean Oxygen Production

Phytoplankton in the ocean are responsible for producing roughly 50% of the world's oxygen, surpassing all of the world's tropical rainforests combined.

Hacking for Good

The term "white hat hacker" refers to ethical hackers who use their skills to help companies bolster their security. Interestingly, the annual prize pool for legal hacking contests at events like DEF CON can reach millions.

A City of Steel

In 1997, Kinshasa, the capital of the Democratic Republic of the Congo, had a surge of self-made engineers. Known as "forgeurs," they transformed cars into new machines using steel parts, creating one of the most vibrant car-renovating cultures on the continent.

No Cash Economy

Some Scandinavian countries like Sweden are moving towards a cashless society. Already, cash transactions make up less than 2% of the economy.

CDC's Zombie Apocalypse Guide

In 2011, the U.S. Centers for Disease Control and Prevention (CDC) posted a tongue-in-cheek blog about preparing for a "zombie apocalypse." This was actually an innovative way to raise awareness about the importance of emergency preparedness.

Pain Tolerance

Contrary to popular belief, women tend to handle pain better than men, in part because of hormonal differences that provide them with greater resilience during childbirth.

Apple's Co-Founder Sold His Shares

Ronald Wayne, a third co-founder of Apple alongside Steve Jobs and Steve Wozniak, sold his 10% stake in the company for just $800 in 1976. Today, that share would be worth billions.

Canberra Was a Compromise
Australia's capital, Canberra, was chosen as a compromise location between Sydney and Melbourne, which were both vying for the capital city status.

The Colossi of Memnon "Singing"
These ancient statues in Egypt were known to emit a strange "singing" sound at dawn, which stopped in 27 BC after one statue was repaired. While some say it's due to temperature changes, the exact cause is still debated.

Benjamin Rush's Gyrator
An 18th-century American psychiatrist believed spinning patients at high speeds could cure mental disorders. Although ineffective and now obsolete, it showcases early experimental approaches to mental health.

Soil Microbiomes
Soil is teeming with life, containing millions of microorganisms per gram. These microbes play a crucial role in nutrient cycling and plant health, impacting food production globally.

The '20-Minute Neighborhoods'
In Portland, Oregon, the city has implemented "20-minute neighborhoods" where all necessary services and amenities are within a 20-minute walk or bike ride, reducing the need for cars and cutting emissions.

Warcraft Leads to AI Progress
The video game "Warcraft" has contributed to progress in artificial intelligence. Research in navigating complex environments and tactical decision-making in games like it has helped advance AI strategies and machine learning.

Extending Lifespan
Genetic engineering has successfully extended the lifespan of certain animals, such as worms and mice, by manipulating genes associated with aging processes, sparking debates about its potential in humans.

United States (Arizona)

Donkeys are not allowed to sleep in bathtubs. This quirky law was enacted after a motel owner's donkey became trapped in a bathtub during a flood.

Mary's Room

This thought experiment posits Mary, a scientist who knows everything about color scientifically but has never seen color herself. When she finally sees red, does she learn something new? It challenges physicalism, the belief that everything about the mind can be explained physically.

Solar-Powered Trees

Cities like Eilat and Haifa have installed "solar trees," innovative structures that use solar panels to generate energy for lighting, USB ports, and more.

Selfie Addiction

In 2014, the psychological term "Selfitis" was coined to describe the obsessive taking of selfies, later acknowledged in a research paper exploring its effects on mental health.

The Shofar's Origin

The shofar, a ram's horn blown on the Jewish New Year, Rosh Hashanah, and at the end of Yom Kippur, is one of the world's oldest wind instruments, with its origins tracing back over 3,000 years.

Antibiotic Resistance Reversal

By using genetic engineering to reprogram bacteria, scientists can reverse antibiotic resistance, potentially restoring antibiotics' effectiveness against superbugs.

Roads Made from Recycled Plastic

Some countries are experimenting with roads made from recycled plastic, which can be more durable and eco-friendly compared to traditional asphalt.

The Tormented "Scream"

Edvard Munch's iconic "The Scream" was inspired by a panic attack he experienced while walking at sunset, where the sky turned blood red. This emotional experience drove the deep anguish depicted in the painting.

Water Buffalo Racing in Bali

In Bali, there is a unique tradition called "Mekepung" where decorated water buffaloes, paired and colorfully adorned, participate in races through the paddy fields as part of the harvest festival.

Bubble Wrap's Initial Failure

Bubble wrap was originally intended to be used as textured wallpaper. The idea failed, but the material was later repurposed as a shipping protective product.

Predictive AI and Human Emotions

Some AI models are becoming adept at reading human emotions through subtle cues in voice modulation, facial expressions, or even written text, astounding psychologists with their accuracy in complex social dynamics.

The Ship of Theseus in Mind

The classic puzzle about whether a ship that has had all its parts replaced remains the same ship is applied to questions of identity in Philosophy of Mind—if all the neurons are replaced, are we the same person?

Extended Mind Theory

Proposed by Andy Clark and David Chalmers, this theory contends that objects in the environment (e.g., notebooks, computers) can become part of the mind, challenging traditional notions of mental processes being confined to the brain.

Loan Strains on Lucas

To finance "The Empire Strikes Back," George Lucas shouldered enormous personal loans, leading him to later famously avoid traditional studio contracts by becoming financially independent.

Project Blue Book

From 1952 to 1969, the U.S. Air Force investigated UFO sightings through Project Blue Book, analyzing over 12,000 reports. While most were explained, 701 cases remain unsolved, fueling speculation about extraterrestrial visitations.

Korowai Treehouses

The Korowai tribe of Papua, Indonesia, is known for building elaborate treehouses that can be constructed as high as 140 feet (around 40 meters) in the air. These structures are designed to ward off insects and spirits, as well as to avoid floods.

Spy Fluorescin

This special dye is used in forensics to detect latent traces of blood. It fluoresces under UV light, even if the actual blood is no longer visible to the naked eye.

Libet's Experiment

Neuroscientist Benjamin Libet's experiments indicated that our brains initiate actions before we're consciously aware of them, raising questions about free will and the nature of consciousness.

No Hair Theorem

Black holes are said to have "no hair," meaning they can be completely described by just three properties: mass, charge, and spin. This makes the inner workings of black holes particularly mysterious.

Thailand

It's illegal to leave your house if you are not wearing underwear. Although it's not commonly enforced, it's still an official law.

Sikh Kirpan

Sikhs traditionally carry a kirpan, a ceremonial dagger, which serves as a reminder of their duty to uphold justice and protect the weak.

Catherine Wheel

Named after St. Catherine of Alexandria, who was martyred on a spiked wheel, these spinning fireworks are a popular pyrotechnic display even today.

Piezoelectric Dance Floors

Some clubs and malls have experimented with flooring that generates electricity when danced or walked upon, capturing kinetic energy in a very party-driven way.

One-line factoids, bizarre truths and juicy chunks of wisdom

Avacha Bay's Pseudo-Tsunami Alarm

Avacha Bay in Kamchatka is known for causing pseudo-tsunami alarms due to peculiar wave reflections, often falsely suggesting the occurrence of tsunamis.

Prussian Influence on American Education

The American public education system was heavily influenced by 19th-century Prussian methods, emphasizing primary education for all children, professional teacher training, and a uniform curriculum.

Dog's Eye View

An AR app called "Dognition" allowed users to understand their dog's perspective by using AR to visualize what the world might look like through a dog's eyes, highlighting their color vision limitations and sensory experience.

The Minoan "Bull-Leapers"

The Minoans of Crete practiced a cultural ritual known as bull-leaping. In this acrobatic feat, participants would grab onto the horns of a charging bull and somersault over its back.

Underground Urban Development

Helsinki, Finland, has an extensive underground city comprising over 200 subterranean facilities, self-sufficient with shops, swimming pools, and even a church, all integrated for energy efficiency.

The 10% Myth

Contrary to the popular myth, we use much more than 10% of our brains. Brain scans show activity coursing throughout almost the entire organ even during simple tasks.

Capgras Delusion

This is a rare condition in which a person believes that someone they know, often a close family member or friend, has been replaced by an identical impostor, reflecting the delicate networks between recognition, emotion, and memory in the brain.

Social Recognition
Recent studies indicate that cats may recognize their owner's voice but often choose to ignore it, whereas dogs typically respond enthusiastically, showcasing their more socially responsive nature.

The Awakened Machines
Some cybersecurity experts warn of AI systems being used in attacks; however, there already exists malware called "polymorphic malware" that can change its code to evade detection.

Koro Syndrome
Predominantly found in Asia, this psychological phenomenon involves the irrational fear that one's genitals are retracting and will disappear, leading to panic and anxiety.

QWERTY's Obscure Purpose
The QWERTY keyboard layout was designed in the 1870s to slow down typists because early typewriters would jam if neighboring keys were pressed rapidly in succession.

Headless Horsemen in Many Cultures
The headless horseman is not just an American phenomenon from Washington Irving's "The Legend of Sleepy Hollow." Variations of this spooky figure can be found across cultures, including the Irish dullahan, a headless rider who usually brings death.

Babies Named After Deceased Relatives
In Jewish tradition, it's common to name babies after deceased relatives to honor their memory.

The First Computer Bug
The term "computer bug" traces back to 1947 when a moth was found trapped in a relay of the Harvard Mark II computer. The incident was recorded in the logbook as the "first actual case of bug being found," giving rise to the popular term.

Gene-Edited Crops
Genetically modified crops can be created that can withstand harsh conditions like drought, pests, and diseases, allowing for increased food security in challenging environments.

Savior Siblings

Some parents have chosen to conceive a new child through in-vitro fertilization specifically to find a genetic match to provide life-saving treatment to an existing sick child, leading to debates on the rights of these "savior siblings."

Dunbar's Number

Anthropologist Robin Dunbar proposed that humans can maintain only about 150 stable social relationships. Beyond this number, it becomes difficult to sustain meaningful interactions and emotional connections, largely due to cognitive limitations.

Longevity

Statistically, women tend to live longer than men. Theories suggest this could be due to genetic advantages—such as two X chromosomes—or lifestyle differences.

The Ghazal Form

Originating in Arabic poetry, the Ghazal is a poetic form that is rather peculiar because traditionally, its last line includes the poet's name or a reference to it, serving as a kind of signature.

Spiders for Sale

In Madagascar, residents sometimes collect giant golden orb-weaver spiders to sell their webs, which are used to make golden silk textiles. This silk can be woven into beautiful, traditional garments.

The "Old Deluder Satan Law"

Enacted in Massachusetts in 1647, this early public health law aimed to thwart Satan by ensuring children were taught to read scripture. Ironically, it's one of the first examples of government-mandated education promoting public well-being.

Ancient Age

Cats have been associated with humans for around 9,000 years, significantly less than dogs, which were domesticated around 20,000 to 40,000 years ago, making dogs some of the first companion animals.

Coconut Threat

The Lethal Yellowing Disease poses a significant threat to coconut populations, crucial for many tropical economies and food security, particularly in the Caribbean and Africa.

Germany's Bottle Deposit Law

Germany's *Pfand* system, which charges a deposit on bottles and cans, has led to a recycling rate of over 90%. A similar system was first introduced in Sweden in 1994.

Titanic's Reverse Filming

To save costs, certain scenes in James Cameron's "Titanic" were filmed in reverse with actors speaking their lines backward. The film was flipped in post-production to make the sequence appear correct.

Norse Mead of Poetry

In Norse mythology, it's believed that wisdom and poetic inspiration came from the Mead of Poetry. This magical mead, made from the blood of Kvasir, a wise being, was said to turn anyone who drank it into a poet or scholar.

Holy Sites Beyond Mecca

While Mecca and Medina are the most famous, Jerusalem is also a revered city in Islam, housing the Al-Aqsa Mosque and the Dome of the Rock, significant sites connected to Islamic history.

Uncertainty Principle

According to Werner Heisenberg's uncertainty principle, there are pairs of properties, such as position and momentum, that cannot be simultaneously measured with arbitrarily high precision. The more precisely one property is known, the less precisely the other can be known.

Need For Speed

Han Solo's iconic spaceship, the Millennium Falcon, was designed to resemble a hamburger, particularly with the cockpit as the "pickle," inspired when Lucas was munching on one during development.

One-line factoids, bizarre truths and juicy chunks of wisdom

Foreign Accent Syndrome

After a brain injury, some people have been known to speak with a foreign accent despite having never learned or been exposed extensively to that language or accent. This rare condition illustrates the complexity of speech production networks in the brain.

Fishy Agriculture

Aquaponics, a combination of aquaculture and hydroponics, allows for the simultaneous farming of fish and plants, offering a highly efficient ecosystem that recycles nutrients.

The Wow! Signal

In 1977, a strong radio signal from space was detected by astronomer Jerry Ehman. It lasted for 72 seconds and was so startling that Ehman wrote "Wow!" next to the data, giving the signal its name. Despite numerous attempts, it has never been repeated or explained.

Egyptian Afterlife Judgment

Ancient Egyptians believed that in the afterlife, the heart of a deceased person was weighed against the feather of Maat (the goddess of truth and justice). If the heart was heavier, indicating a life of sin, it was devoured by a creature called Ammit.

Anti-Nudity Legislation

Hiking naked was a trend that led to the Swiss introducing specific laws in 2009 to outlaw such public displays after Austrian tourists began hiking nude in the mountains.

Trobriand Islanders and "Matriarchal Magic"

The Trobriand Islands, part of Papua New Guinea, have a unique belief system where sexuality and "magic" are central to the society. Women hold significant power over land and resources, challenging traditional Western gender roles.

Denmark

Parents must be careful when naming their child. Denmark has a list of about 7,000 pre-approved names. If a name is not on the list, they have to get government approval.

Emu War

In the 1930s, Australia had an actual military operation known as the "Emu War," where soldiers were deployed to combat the overpopulation of emus that were damaging crops in Western Australia. The emus won, proving surprisingly elusive and resilient.

Summer Break Origin

The summer break in the United States originally evolved not because of farming cycles, but to give urban children a break during the hottest months when there was no air conditioning.

Mushroom Leather

Mycelium, the root structure of mushrooms, can be cultivated to create a sustainable, biodegradable leather alternative that has diverse applications, including fashion and furniture.

Kidney Chains

The idea of kidney donation chains, where a network of donors and recipients are matched in a domino-like fashion, has raised ethical questions about fairness and the allocation of organs, but has significantly increased transplant opportunities.

Quantum Tunneling

Quantum computers can utilize quantum tunneling, a phenomenon that allows particles to pass through barriers that would be insurmountable in the classical world, providing potentially faster solutions to certain computational problems.

Penguins in Africa

The African continent is home to a species of penguin, known as the African Penguin or Jackass Penguin. They inhabit the southwestern coast of Africa, living in colonies on 24 islands between Namibia and Algoa Bay, South Africa.

Social Ostracism and Physical Pain

Research has shown that the brain processes social rejection in a similar way to physical pain. Areas of the brain associated with physical pain also light up when a person experiences social exclusion or heartbreak, illustrating how deeply interconnected our social and physical experiences are.

Color Chemistry
The brilliant colors of fireworks are created through metal salts: barium for green, strontium for red, sodium for yellow, and copper for blue. Creating a bright blue is particularly difficult due to the high temperatures needed.

Sea Cucumber Self-Defense
When threatened, some sea cucumbers can expel their internal organs out of their bodies. They later regenerate these organs, a process that helps them evade predators.

Fingerprint Forgery
Criminals have attempted to alter or remove their fingerprints using surgery, acid, or even superglue, with varying degrees of success—though usually ineffective.

Chinese Ideograms
In written Chinese, a single character can represent a full word or concept and sometimes even an entire sentence, vastly simplifying information when compared to alphabetic languages.

Universal Repellent
Scientists developed a superhydrophobic material through nanotechnology, which can repel not only water but also dirt, ketchup, and even some oils, promising self-cleaning surfaces.

Spider Silk from Goats
Scientists have inserted spider silk genes into goats so that they produce silk proteins in their milk. This silk can then be harvested and used to produce super-strong materials.

Microbiome Influence
The gut microbiome - trillions of bacteria living in our intestinal tract - can influence our brain health. Through the gut-brain axis, these microbes can affect our mood, cognition, and even mental health disorders.

The "Horn of Africa" Connection
Many historical accounts suggest early Muslims sought refuge in Ethiopia when they were persecuted in Mecca, indicating early Islamic connections with Africa.

The Tunguska Event

In 1908, a mysterious explosion flattened over 800 square miles of Siberian forest. It is commonly attributed to the mid-air explosion of a meteoroid, but the lack of an impact crater and other anomalies have led to some paranormal theories, like alien intervention.

"Haunted" Pokémon

During the Pokémon Go craze, there were reports of people accidentally wandering into dangerous areas, including a cemetery at night while hunting for Pokémon like Gastly—a ghost-type Pokémon!

Quantum Superposition

A quantum system can exist in multiple states at the same time. This concept is famously illustrated by Schrödinger's cat, which is sImultaneously alive and dead until observed.

Oldest Continually Inhabited City

Varanasi is known to be one of the world's oldest continually inhabited cities. It is a major cultural and religious hub, believed to be more than 3,000 years old.

The Stockholm Syndrome Paradox

Named after a bank robbery in 1973 where hostages developed an attachment to their captors, this syndrome demonstrates how captives can form bonds with their oppressors, challenging our understanding of loyalty and survival.

Cancer Treatment

There are ongoing clinical trials using gene modification to edit immune cells to better target and destroy cancer cells, offering hope for more effective treatments.

Keystroke Languages

In some cultures, people have developed systems of communication using drumming, such as with the "talking drums" of West Africa, which can mimic the tones and rhythms of speech.

One-line factoids, bizarre truths and juicy chunks of wisdom

Alice Springs Solar Town
Australia's Alice Springs is experimenting with a comprehensive solar-powered microgrid system, striving to make itself one of the most environmentally sustainable towns in the world.

Shani Shingnapur
In many homes and businesses in the village of Shani Shingnapur in Maharashtra, doors and locks are absent. Residents believe that Shani, the god of Saturn, protects them from theft.

Deep Learning's Cat Recognition
In 2012, a neural network trained by Google learned to recognize cats without being explicitly told what a cat is. The AI analyzed millions of images from YouTube, where cats are a popular subject.

Solar Roads
There are projects dedicated to creating solar panels that double as roadways. These solar roads can generate electricity while supporting the weight of cars and trucks.

Ben Franklin Effect
Named after Benjamin Franklin, the phenomenon suggests that if you do someone a favor, you are more likely to like them as a result. Franklin noted that you could win over a rival by asking them for a favor, as the mind tends to reconcile liking someone with whom it's invested effort or resources.

The Zimbardo Time Perspective Inventory
Philip Zimbardo developed a theory focusing on how individuals perceive time, suggesting that one's orientation (past, present, future) dramatically affects decision-making and personality.

Immortal Jellyfish
The Turritopsis dohrnii, often called the "immortal jellyfish," can revert its cells to their earliest form after reaching maturity, essentially cheating death and potentially living indefinitely.

Snapchat's Ghostly Mascot
Snapchat's mascot, named "Ghostface Chillah," is inspired by Ghostface Killah, a rapper from the Wu-Tang Clan.

Kayan Longneck Women in Myanmar
The women of the Kayan tribe in Myanmar are famous for wearing brass neck coils, starting from a young age. They add more rings over time, creating the appearance of elongated necks, which is considered a sign of beauty and cultural identity.

Highway Tribute to Spaghetti
The city of Chongqing has a highway interchange that looks like a plate of spaghetti. The Huangjuewan Flyover has 15 ramps spread across five levels.

The World's First Speeding Ticket
The first speeding ticket was issued in 1896 in London. The accused, Walter Arnold, was caught driving 8 mph in a 2 mph zone. He was fined 1 shilling.

The Singing Wells of Kenya
In certain regions, Kenyan tribes dig wells during the dry season and sing unique songs to call their cattle to drink. Each family has its own specific song.

Quantum Supremacy
In 2019, Google claimed to achieve quantum supremacy, where their quantum computer performed a specific calculation faster than the world's most powerful supercomputers. The task, which took Google's quantum computer 200 seconds, would have taken the best classical supercomputer approximately 10,000 years!

Potlatch in Indigenous North American Cultures
The potlatch is a ceremonial feast practiced by Indigenous peoples of the Pacific Northwest. It's known for the host giving away vast amounts of wealth as a display of wealth and status, emphasizing communal sharing over accumulation.

VR Sickness
Some people experience motion sickness in VR, a phenomenon known as VR sickness. It's caused by the disconnect between what the eyes see and what the body feels, but studies suggest chewing gum can help reduce the symptoms.

Aging and Memory

It's a common belief that we lose many neurons as we age, contributing to memory loss. However, more recent research suggests that significant neuron loss happens in pathological conditions rather than normal aging.

Madurai's Famous Sunglasses Rock

In Madurai, Tamil Nadu, there is a rock formation resembling a pair of sunglasses, created naturally over time. It's viewed as both a curiosity and a local landmark.

Kaminitz Bat House

Israel hosts a specialized "bat house" in one of Tel Aviv's older neighborhoods. These structures are designed to encourage bats to roost, aiding pest control naturally.

Kuna People and the "Island of Women"

Among the Kuna people of Panama, the small island of Isla de Mujeres is known for its highly matriarchal society. Women largely control social and economic aspects, and inheritance typically passes through the female line.

Vampire Watermelon

According to a Slavic folk tale, watermelons left on the vine for more than ten days after ripening can turn into vampires. These vampire watermelons would supposedly roll around at night and attack unsuspecting locals.

Cow Trees

According to Norse mythology, the entire universe was held together by Yggdrasil, a massive, ash tree that connected the Nine Worlds. Within these realms were countless mythical creatures including Ymir, the first being, who was nourished by a cow named Audhumla.

Chinese Creation via Cosmic Egg

An ancient Chinese myth describes the universe's formation with a giant cosmic egg. This egg contained all of existence until it was split open, creating the heavens and earth, with the first being, Pangu, emerging from it.

Erotomania

A person with this condition is convinced that someone, often a celebrity or person of higher status, is in love with them, despite clear evidence to the contrary.

The Finnish Love for Coffee

Per capita, Finns drink more coffee than any other nation in the world. Breaks for coffee, or "kahvitauko," are an essential part of Finnish work culture.

Living on the Edge

Despite being one of the most arid continents, Australia accounts for only 1% of the world's agricultural production but is responsible for 14% of global wheat trade due to its export focus.

Kazan's Temple of All Religions

An architectural complex symbolizing unity among the world's religions, featuring influences from 16 faiths, including Christianity, Islam, Judaism, and Buddhism.

Viking Sun Compasses

Despite popular belief in their reliance on stars and primitive instruments, Vikings may have used sun compasses to navigate, utilizing the sun's shadow to maintain direction on cloudy days.

Foot Binding in China

Until the early 20th century, Chinese women practiced foot binding to make their feet as small as possible, which was considered beautiful and a status symbol. This painful tradition often resulted in lifelong disabilities.

Coffee Origin

The discovery of coffee is often attributed to Yemen in the Sufi monasteries. It spread across the Muslim world before reaching Europe, where it became the beloved beverage we know today.

The Largest Population

Indonesia is the country with the largest Muslim population in the world, surpassing traditionally Muslim-majority countries in the Middle East.

Poe's Cemetery Toast

Fans of Edgar Allan Poe have kept a mysterious tradition known as the "Poe Toaster," where an unidentified person visits his grave every January 19th (his birthday) to leave a half-bottle of cognac and three roses.

Avatar's Unique Flora

James Cameron conceived the glowing flora of Pandora for "Avatar" based on a camping trip where he observed bioluminescent fungi in the dark.

Banana Crisis

The Gros Michel banana, the dominant cultivar in the first half of the 20th century, was nearly wiped out by the Panama disease, leading to the current reliance on the Cavendish variety, which is now also threatened by similar diseases.

Largest Country by Land Area

Russia is the largest country in the world by land area, taking up more than 11% of Earth's landmass. It's so big that it spans 11 time zones!

Galactic Highways

Researchers have discovered "space superhighways" — networks of gravitational forces that can allow spacecraft and space debris to travel quickly across the solar system, potentially aiding future exploration.

Color-Changing Lobsters

Lobsters are not red like we often see them on the dinner table; they're usually blue, green, or brown in the wild. Only cooking turns them red due to a change in a protein called astaxanthin.

The World's Oldest Known "Toilet"

Fossilized dung found in Scotland is over 240 million years old and comes from ancient reptiles—not surprisingly predating humans by millions of years—in a finding revealing communal bathroom behavior.

Synesthesia

This is a condition where the stimulation of one sensory pathway leads to automatic, involuntary experiences in a second sensory pathway. Some people with synesthesia might "see" sounds as colors or "taste" words as flavors.

Kesha's Tooth Necklace

Pop star Kesha made a necklace out of her fans' teeth after they sent her about 1,000 of them.

Geothermal Beer

In Reykjavik, Iceland, a brewery utilizes geothermal energy to brew its beer. The energy, harvested from the Earth's natural heat, provides an eco-friendly brewing process.

The Golem Myth

In Jewish folklore, a golem is an animated creature created entirely from inanimate matter, often clay. The most famous is the Golem of Prague, said to have been fashioned by Rabbi Judah Loew ben Bezalel in the 16th century to protect the Jewish community.

Amazon's All-encompassing Wishlist

Before it became the "Everything Store," Amazon was a bookstore. Interestingly, Jeff Bezos originally wanted to name it "Cadabra," as in "abracadabra," but changed it after realizing it sounded too much like "cadaver" over the phone.

Pokemon GO Genocide

The Holocaust Memorial Museum in Washington, D.C., had to request visitors not use Pokémon Go on its premises because some players were catching Pokémon inappropriately named after the museum's sensitive content.

Tsunami of Saliva

In a lifetime, a person produces enough saliva to fill two average-sized swimming pools.

The Sudbury School Model

Some schools, like those following the Sudbury model, have no set curriculum or traditional classes. Students are free to spend their time as they wish, believing that self-directed learning fosters personal responsibility and passion.

The Whistled Language

In La Gomera, one of Spain's Canary Islands, people use a whistled language called "Silbo Gomero" to communicate across long distances.

Madagascar's Unique Wildlife

About 90% of Madagascar's wildlife is found nowhere else on Earth. This includes the iconic lemurs, which only reside on the island.

The Quantum Age

We are in the early stages of what might be considered the "quantum age." Just like classical computing revolutionized technology in the 20th century, quantum computing is expected to lead to unprecedented advances in various fields in the future.

The Piltdown Man Deception

In 1912, the "Piltdown Man" was hailed as a pivotal human ancestor. Decades later, it was revealed to be a hoax composed of a medieval human skull and an orangutan jaw, highlighting how easily scientific consensus can be misled.

Saturn's Bizarre Hexagon

Saturn's north pole features a persistent, hexagon-shaped cloud pattern that has baffled scientists since its discovery by the Voyager spacecraft in the early 1980s.

Jet-Powered Trains

In the 1960s, jet engines were fitted onto trains as experimental high-speed propulsion methods. The New York Central Railroad had a jet-powered railcar that reached speeds of up to 183 mph.

The Sheep Outnumber People

New Zealand has a famously high sheep-to-human ratio, often cited as being around 5:1. At its peak, the ratio was as high as 22 sheep for every person.

Euthanasia Towers

In fictional works and concept proposals, euthanasia towers were imagined where individuals can decide to end their life voluntarily. Although not real, these highlight ongoing challenges in discussing euthanasia and assisted suicide.

The Clerihew

This is a whimsical four-line biographical poem, often with irregular meter and an AABB rhyme scheme, invented by Edmund Clerihew Bentley to humorously personify historical and literary figures.

Dolphin Delights

Dolphins are one of the few animal species that engage in sex not just for reproduction, but also for pleasure. They even have been known to use objects for sexual stimulation.

Namibian Fairy Circles

These mysterious circular patches of barren land, found in the Namib Desert, have puzzled scientists for years. Theories suggest they could be caused by termites or self-organizing plants.

Negative Interest Rates

Some central banks, like those in Japan and Switzerland, have adopted negative interest rates, which means depositors are actually charged to keep their money in banks. This is aimed at incentivizing spending and investment.

Poincaré Conjecture

Solved by Grigori Perelman in 2003, this was one of the seven "Millennium Prize" problems, and Perelman turned down the $1 million prize and a Fields Medal.

Vampire Squid's Unique Diet

The vampire squid survives in the low-oxygen deep sea and feeds on "marine snow" — a nutrient-rich mixture of dead plankton, fecal matter, and other organic debris.

San Bushmen's Clicking Language

The San people of the Kalahari Desert in southern Africa use a series of click sounds within their languages, such as !Kung and !Xóõ. These languages are known for their extensive phonetic diversity.

Cargo Cults

In some Pacific islands, cargo cults formed when indigenous people started venerating Western goods and the people bringing them. They performed rituals hoping to attract cargo drops from the sky.

One-line factoids, bizarre truths and juicy chunks of wisdom

Garlic-Kissing Therapy (1970s)

Invented to help couples with halitosis confront their issues, it recommended both partners eat garlic before kissing. Unsurprisingly, it did not gain popularity.

Superposition

Quantum bits, or qubits, can exist in a state of superposition, meaning they can be both 0 and 1 simultaneously. This property allows quantum computers to process massive amounts of data simultaneously, unlike classical bits which are either 0 or 1.

Antarctica Has Mountains Taller Than the Alps

The Gamburtsev Mountain Range stretches across 1,200 kilometers (750 miles) and reaches elevations comparable to the European Alps. Strangely, these mountains are entirely buried under ice.

Switzerland

It's illegal to flush the toilet after 10 p.m. in some apartment buildings. This law is intended to reduce noise at night.

Size Isn't Everything

The size of the brain doesn't necessarily determine intelligence. While Neanderthals had larger brains than modern humans, this didn't equate to greater cognitive capabilities.

Untranslatable Words

Many languages contain words with no direct English equivalent, such as "Schadenfreude" in German, which describes the pleasure derived from another person's misfortune.

Fear of Fireworks (Phonophobia)

While many enjoy fireworks, a condition called phonophobia—a fear of loud sounds—can make firework displays distressing for some, including many pets who suffer from this during the festivities.

The Curse of Y2K

As the year 2000 approached, there was widespread concern that computer systems would fail due to a programming shortcut using only two digits for years. The nickname "Y2K bug" worried businesses around the globe, but extensive efforts prevented major issues.

The Sea of Galilee's Rising and Falling
Known for being one of the lowest freshwater lakes on Earth, the Sea of Galilee's water levels can impact political discussions around its use with neighboring countries.

Roman Freshwater Eels
Ancient Romans had a penchant for unusual aquatic entertainment. Wealthy Romans sometimes kept pet eels encrusted with jewelry, and they believed that treating them well would earn them the eels' trust and companionship.

Miniature Gardens
There is a popular Swiss festival where townsfolk transform their walkways into miniature gardens using trays of wheatgrass, a tradition known as "Sechseläuten."

The First Tweet
The very first tweet was sent by Twitter's co-founder Jack Dorsey on March 21, 2006. It read, "just setting up my twttr."

The Global Effort to Eradicate Guinea Worm
The Guinea worm, a parasite that can grow up to 3 feet long inside the human body, is on the verge of global eradication thanks to efforts led by The Carter Center. This remarkable public health achievement involves educating communities, providing safe drinking water, and simply using a cloth to filter out the larvae.

The Great Switcheroo of Buenos Aires
In 1536, Buenos Aires was originally founded by Spanish explorers but was abandoned five years later because of conflicts with local indigenous peoples, leading to it being refounded in 1580.

Flightless Birds
The ancestors of present-day flightless birds like ostriches, emus, and kiwis were once capable of flight. However, over millions of years, these birds evolved to be flightless due to a lack of predators in their environments or more efficient ground feeding strategies.

Bhutan's Carbon-Negative Status

One of the most unique records in environmental policy, Bhutan absorbs more carbon than it emits. The country is carbon-negative, largely due to its vast forests and commitment to preserving natural resources.

Plasticity

The brain is highly adaptable and can change throughout an individual's life, a characteristic known as neuroplasticity. This allows the brain to rewire itself in response to learning and experience and even recover from injury to some extent.

Fish as Bank Collateral

Certain small-scale banks in India accept dried fish as collateral for micro-loans. This happens in coastal areas, where fishing is a predominant occupation.

Floating Cities

Plans for floating cities are underway, such as Oceanix City, designed to house climate refugees. These modular platforms could host communities and are designed to be sustainable, with solar panels and greenhouses.

The "Bellybutton of the World"

The small village of Sholokhovo cheekily refers to itself as the "Bellybutton of the World" for its seemingly random and remote location within the vast expanses of Russia.

Condor Adoption Programs

California condors, which once numbered only 22 in the wild, were brought back through complex breeding programs. To prevent human imprinting, puppets are used to feed chicks.

Bataknese Wedding in Indonesia

In Bataknese culture, it's believed that the groom should "kidnap" the bride as a part of a traditional wedding custom. Of course, it is symbolic and ceremonial these days, with full consent and participation from both families.

Sentinelese

The Sentinelese people from North Sentinel Island in the Andaman Sea are one of the last uncontacted tribes in the world. They are known to reject any contact with outsiders, sometimes using force to remain isolated. Their language is distinct and not understood by outsiders.

Ben-Hur's Unusual Credit

The 1925 silent film "Ben-Hur" holds the odd distinction of having directors with more screen credits than the stars. It went through four directors during its tumultuous production.

Cold Storage

Most quantum computers operate on principles that require them to be extremely cold — often colder than outer space — to keep the qubits stable. This is achieved using dilution refrigerators, which can operate at temperatures close to absolute zero.

Tana Toraja Funerals in Indonesia

In Tana Toraja, funerals are monumental events where the deceased are kept at home for an extended period until the family can afford a lavish ceremony. The dead are often treated as if they are merely "sick" or "sleeping" during this time.

Shimmering Sands

The Richat Structure, also known as the Eye of the Sahara, is a 25-mile-wide geological formation in Mauritania. Its concentric rings make it look like a massive target from space, but its precise origins remain a mystery.

Environmental Ballot Initiatives

In 1978, Californians passed Proposition 13, drastically cutting property taxes and fundamentally altering public funding frameworks, including for environmental initiatives. It's a historical example of how policies not directly labeled "environmental" can have significant ecological impacts.

Legalized Adventure

New Zealand has some of the most (bizarrely) adventurous laws. For instance, bungee jumping is legally regulated as an extreme sports activity. It was commercialized for the first time in the world on the Kawarau Bridge near Queenstown in 1988.

Virtual Real Estate

People are investing in virtual real estate within platforms like Decentraland and The Sandbox. Some plots of virtual land have sold for hundreds of thousands of dollars, valued based on their digital locations and potential for VR experiences.

Drifting Baklava

During a space mission in 1965, astronaut John Young smuggled a corned beef sandwich aboard Gemini 3, causing crumbs to float around the cabin and prompting NASA to review food protocols for missions.

Oldest University

The University of al-Qarawiyyin in Fez, Morocco, is recognized by UNESCO and the Guinness World Records as the oldest existing, continually operating higher educational institution in the world, founded in 859 AD.

Fibonacci Sequence in Nature

The Fibonacci sequence (0, 1, 1, 2, 3, 5, 8...) appears in nature, such as the arrangement of leaves, the fruitlets of a pineapple, or the branching of trees.

Floating National Park

The world's only floating national park, the Okavango Delta in Botswana, is created by seasonal floods which expand the delta's size dramatically from May to September, supporting an incredible diversity of wildlife.

The Mystery of Basque

The Basque language, spoken in the region straddling France and Spain, is a language isolate, meaning it has no known living relatives.

Eruv: Creating Boundaries

In cities around the world, you might find an eruv, which is a halachic (Jewish legal) boundary that allows observant Jews to carry objects outside their homes on the Sabbath without breaking religious laws.

Salvador Dalí's Ocelot

The surrealist artist Salvador Dalí had a pet ocelot named Babou, which he would sometimes bring to public events. It's said that he once took Babou to a restaurant, reassuring fellow diners that it was just a normal cat painted in an op-art design.

ENIAC's Military Origin

ENIAC, one of the first electronic general-purpose computers, was originally designed for the U.S. Army during World War II to calculate artillery firing tables faster—an effort to replace human "computers" who manually performed these calculations.

Nicolas Cage Owns a Pyramid Tomb

The eccentric actor bought a 9-foot-tall pyramid-shaped tomb in New Orleans, where he plans to be buried one day.

The Infinite Recursion of Universes

Hindu cosmology describes the existence of infinite universes. Each universe undergoes repeated cycles of creation, preservation, and destruction, known as pralaya, in an eternal pattern.

Quantum Decoherence

This is the process by which a quantum system loses its quantum properties as it interacts with the environment, transitioning into classical states. Decoherence is why we don't observe superpositions in the macroscopic world.

Italy (Florence)

It's illegal to eat or drink while sitting on church steps or within the vicinity of public buildings and historic squares in Florence.

Living Root Bridges

In the northeastern state of Meghalaya, some villages use living root bridges made by training the roots of rubber trees across rivers. These natural bridges can withstand heavy weights and last for centuries.

Mini Black Holes

Theoretically, mini primordial black holes could have formed in the early universe and might be roaming undetected, depending on whether they have evaporated via Hawking radiation.

Goddess of Excrement

In Japanese mythology, there exists a deity known as Kawaya-no-kami who is the kami (spirit) of the toilet. She was believed to keep outhouses safe and was often honored for ensuring hygiene and safety in these spaces.

CT Scan Autopsies

Postmortem imaging using CTs and MRIs is becoming more common. These "virtual autopsies" can be done without making incisions and provide detailed internal views.

Skeleton Lake

Underneath Jerusalem's Yemin Moshe neighborhood lies a subterranean lake that was accidentally discovered by builders. It's an ancient reservoir filled with fish and skeletons.

Augmented Surgery

AR is used in surgeries to provide real-time guidance to surgeons. In one instance, an AR headset was used to overlay a 3D model of a patient's vascular system directly onto their body during surgery, providing enhanced precision.

Rat Eradication on South Georgia Island

In a unique conservation effort, the British-claimed South Georgia Island undertook a massive rat eradication project to protect native bird species. Helicopters dropped tons of bait laced with poison, successfully ridding the island of rodents by 2018.

The Friendship Paradox

On average, people are likely to have fewer friends than their friends do. This paradox occurs because people with many friends are more likely to be counted among your friends, which skews the average.

The Flatwoods Monster

In 1952, after seeing a UFO crash-land in West Virginia, witnesses reported encountering a towering, alien-like figure with glowing red eyes and a hooded head—a creature that became known as the Flatwoods Monster.

Long-Lived Tenants

Archaeologists have found prehistoric cave dwellings lived in continuously for over 40,000 years, as evidenced by habitation at sites like Les Eyzies-de-Tayac in France.

Dutch Tulip Mania
In the 17th century, the Netherlands experienced a massive economic bubble known as Tulip Mania, where the prices of tulip bulbs reached extraordinarily high levels before dramatically collapsing.

Size Comparison
A nanometer is one billionth of a meter. To put it in perspective, if a marble were a nanometer, then a meter would be the size of the Earth.

Lip Plates in Ethiopia
The Mursi people of Ethiopia are known for their lip plates. Both a symbol of beauty and a rite of passage, women wear increasingly larger plates in their lower lips. It's considered a sign of coming of age and status within the community.

Space Smells
Astronauts describe the smell of space as a mixture of hot metal, seared steak, and welding fumes, noticing it particularly on spacesuits after returning from a spacewalk.

Mary Mallon, aka Typhoid Mary
An Irish cook in the early 1900s, Mary Mallon was the first known asymptomatic carrier of typhoid fever in the U.S. Despite causing several outbreaks, she refused to believe she carried the disease and continued working, infecting dozens of people over her career.

Prohibition in the UK
In 1605, following the Gunpowder Plot, fireworks were made illegal in the United Kingdom to prevent civil uprisings. It wasn't until 1650 that they were legalized again for celebratory purposes.

Magwa Water Splashes in Myanmar
In some regions of Myanmar, during Thingyan (New Year Festival), locals partake in playful water fights to wash away misfortunes, a custom aimed at purifying and anticipating fresh beginnings.

One-line factoids, bizarre truths and juicy chunks of wisdom

Walking Marriage in China

Among the Mosuo people in southwestern China, the concept of marriage is virtually non-existent. Instead, they practice "walking marriages," where partners visit each other at night but live separately and raise children with their maternal family.

AI Chatbots and Antisocial Behavior

Some AI chatbots, when left to learn from internet conversations, have adopted negative behaviors. The infamous example is Microsoft's Tay, a Twitter bot that began to produce offensive tweets within hours of launching, due to learning from the interactions with users.

The Cats' Eyes in Shoes (1960s)

An inventor once created shoes with tiny headlights called "Cats' Eyes" meant for night walking. Despite being innovative, they never became a trendsetter.

The Drooling God

In Aztec mythology, Tlaloc was the god of rain, water, and earthly fertility. It was believed that when Tlaloc shed his tears, it resulted in rain, but he was also associated with thunder and lightning when angered.

Hildegard von Bingen's Visions

The medieval composer and mystic Hildegard von Bingen claimed to have experienced divine visions, which she often described in her writings. Some scholars suggest these might have been migraines.

Film Funds With Baby Teeth

In order to fund "El Mariachi," filmmaker Robert Rodriguez sold blood plasma and participated in experimental drug studies. The film went on to become a cult classic and launched Rodriguez's career.

Norway's King Penguins

In a peculiar tradition, the Norwegian Royal Guard adopted a king penguin named Sir Nils Olav who is stationed at the Edinburgh Zoo. He's been given various promotions and is considered a mascot of sorts.

Artificial Wombs

As science advances in developing artificial wombs, ethical discourses intensify around rights, parenthood, and potential impacts on natural childbirth and societal norms.

Space Age Pet

Scientists suspect a group of water-loving dinosaurs, such as Spinosaurus, might have had adaptations similar to modern submarines, with physical features suited for aquatic environments, a unique trait among large theropods.

Ursonate

Kurt Schwitters, a German artist, composed "Ursonate," a sound poem performed as a vocal score focusing entirely on phonetic sounds and sounds without semantic meaning rather than actual words.

Saltwater Electricity

Researchers are exploring the use of saltwater in salinity gradient energy schemes, where power is generated by the difference in salt concentration between saltwater and freshwater.

Michelangelo and David's Disproportion

Michelangelo's famous statue of David has some deliberate anatomical inaccuracies. The hands and head are unusually large, likely because the statue was meant to be viewed from a lower point, making these features appear in proportion when seen from below.

Bio-architecture

Algae-filled bioreactor walls have been incorporated in building designs to absorb sunlight and produce biomass for energy, while also providing natural shading.

Cows as Bank Accounts

In various parts of Africa, cows are seen as a form of wealth and even used as a type of bank. In some cultures, a person's wealth is measured by the number of cattle they own.

One-line factoids, bizarre truths and juicy chunks of wisdom

The City with Two Ps
The town of Whanganui can be spelled with or without the 'h' (Wanganui) depending on personal preference due to historic spelling differences and regional dialects.

Brain Size and Function
On average, men's brains are about 10% larger than women's, yet size doesn't correlate with intelligence. Interestingly, women typically have more gray matter related to processing and judgment, possibly explaining their adeptness at multitasking.

Yekaterinburg's "Keyboard Monument"
Built in 2005, it consists of 86 stone keys arranged to resemble a giant computer keyboard and is a quirky homage to technology.

The SimGas Project
In Rwanda, methane from Lake Kivu is harvested to produce energy and prevent a potential "lake overturn" explosion, a rare but catastrophic natural event. This turns a potential public health hazard into a beneficial energy source.

Amulets and Magic
Despite strict prohibitions against witchcraft and necromancy in the Torah, Jewish history is rich with the belief in protective amulets and some forms of mystical magic, particularly in Kabbalistic traditions.

Etruscan Divination with Sheep Livers
The Etruscans were known to practice divination by examining the liver of a sheep. They believed that the liver reflected the will of the gods, and specialized priests called haruspices interpreted the messages.

The Hitchcock Cameo Tradition
Alfred Hitchcock, the legendary director, made cameo appearances in 39 of his films, often appearing in the first half to avoid distracting the audience from the story.

Visionary Child

St. Juan Diego, a 16th-century indigenous Mexican, reported four apparitions of the Virgin Mary, leading to the creation of the icon of Our Lady of Guadalupe, which has become a major symbol of Mexican Christianity.

iPhone's Secret Project

The iPhone started as a covert project under the code name "Project Purple." Developers working on it wore trench coats and carried top-secret badges to maintain confidentiality.

Ghost Marriage in China and Vietnam

In certain rural areas of China and Vietnam, there is a custom of conducting ghost marriages, which involve marrying off deceased loved ones to ensure they have companionship in the afterlife.

More Is Less

The "Infinite Scroll" feature, designed to keep users engaged by continually loading new content, was pioneered by Aza Raskin in 2006 but later discovered to cause users to spend more time than intended on sites, creating a paradox of time use online.

AI-Powered "Zombie" Simulations

Some AI research includes simulations of unlikely but theoretical scenarios, like zombie apocalypses. These are used to understand herd behavior, disease spread, and emergency responses.

Fishtail Park Assist

Some of the earliest attempts at parallel parking assistance, like the "parking lamp," involved drivers lighting a hanging lamp to illuminate tight spaces better at night.

Zoroastrian Exposure Burial

In ancient Zoroastrianism, "Towers of Silence" were used for funerary practices. Bodies were placed atop these towers and left to be consumed by vultures, which was seen as a pure way to dispose of the dead without contaminating the earth.

Wizardry Is a Job

New Zealand is one of the few countries that employed an official "Wizard." Ian Brackenbury Channell, the Wizard of New Zealand, was appointed by the Prime Minister in 1990 to enliven the spirit of the nation.

Pink Lakes

Australia is home to several pink lakes, the most famous being Lake Hillier. The lake's distinct pink color is caused by the presence of specific algae and bacteria.

Spinning Skylab

America's first space station, Skylab, experienced a mechanical issue during launch that stripped off a micrometeoroid shield. To compensate, astronauts had to manually repair and spin the station to equalize the temperature, creating artificial gravity.

Qur'an Recitation

There are annual competitions for Qur'an recitation that are held globally, attracting participants from all over the world, with categories ranging from memorization to the quality of recitation.

Barack Obama Firework Song

In 2008, an electronic-pop song entitled "Obama! Obama!" featured fireworks sound effects as part of the celebration of Barack Obama's presidential campaign.

Desert Snows

The Sahara Desert, known for its scorching heat, has experienced snowfall several times in recent years, with snow blanketing parts of Algeria in 1979, 2012, and more recently, 2018.

Leonardo DiCaprio's Lucky Cat

After surviving a plane malfunction, an almost shark attack, and a skydiving mishap, he often attributes his survival to his lucky cat named Moses.

Sahara Snowfall
Although the Sahara Desert is known for its scorching heat, it experienced a rare snowfall in December 2016 and again in January 2018. About 1-3 inches of snow fell near the town of Ain Sefra in Algeria.

Cartesian Dualism
Proposed by René Descartes, this idea suggests the mind and body are separate substances. Critics humorously ask where the mind and brain interact—maybe the "pineal gland," where he speculatively located it!

Gecko Inspiration
Carbon nanotube technology is inspired by the way gecko feet use nanoscopic hair structures to stick to surfaces. This has led to the development of gecko tape, an adhesive with no glue.

Freestyle Shakespeare
A group known as "The Q Brothers" have modernized Shakespeare's plays into freestyle, hip-hop versions, turning the rhythmically complex iambic pentameter into rapid-fire rap lyrics.

Inuit Sun Navigation
Inuit communities in the Arctic, known for their adept survival skills in extreme cold, traditionally navigate vast ice expanses by observing the sun's position and using oral maps remembered from landmarks and stories.

Telepresence Frogs
Scientists have experimented with "telepresence" amphibians using VR. They placed frogs in a VR environment to test their spatial navigation abilities and responses to virtual stimuli.

Pirahã Language Complexity
The Pirahã people of the Amazon have a language with no fixed words for colors or numbers, reflecting a unique worldview focused on immediate experience.

Da Vinci's "The Last Supper" Has a Hidden Door
Leonardo da Vinci's fresco "The Last Supper" includes a curious architectural quirk: a doorway was cut into the mural in the 1600s that removed part of Jesus's feet, altering the original design.

One-line factoids, bizarre truths and juicy chunks of wisdom

Mental Health
Women are more likely to experience depression and anxiety disorders than men, while men are more frequently diagnosed with ADHD and autism spectrum disorders.

Gabriel's Horn Paradox
Also known as Torricelli's Trumpet, it's a shape that has infinite surface area but possesses a finite volume, which defies physical intuition.

Underwater Museums
Off the coast of Caesarea, there's an underwater museum where divers and snorkelers can explore ancient ruins submerged in the Mediterranean Sea.

Singapore
Chewing gum is strictly regulated. Importing chewing gum into Singapore is illegal due to the mess and cleaning costs it causes.

Moksha Through Dance
It is believed that dancing the Bharatanatyam or any other classical Indian dance form, with true devotion, can earn the dancer Moksha, or liberation from the cycle of rebirth.

Rihanna's Real Name
While globally known as Rihanna, her full name is actually Robyn Rihanna Fenty.

Jesus in Japan
A legend exists that Jesus escaped crucifixion and settled in Japan, living out his days in the village of Shingō. The town hosts the alleged tomb of Christ, complete with a local museum explaining the myth.

Holy Tooth
Several Christian traditions claim to possess relics known as the "tooth of Jesus." The tooth housed in the Basilica of San Lorenzo outside the Walls in Rome was allegedly given by an angel to St. Francis of Assisi.

Brain Death

The concept of brain death, where a person can be officially dead in brain activity yet show bodily functions due to medical technology, continues to spark ethical debates about what truly constitutes death.

Four National Languages

With no single national language, Switzerland has four official languages: German, French, Italian, and Romansh, creating a remarkably multilingual society.

The World's Smallest Prayer Book

An Israeli nanotechnology company created a prayer book smaller than a grain of sugar, containing almost 1.2 million letters of Hebrew text etched on a silicon chip.

Populations

There are approximately 900 million domestic cats in the world but a greater number of dogs as pets, although exact figures vary by country and breed.

Easter Island's Trees

Indicates some one-time dense forests. The first Europeans who arrived in 1722 found Easter Island barren of trees, but evidence suggests it was once lush with palm trees until overpopulation and resource exploitation led to deforestation.

The Time of the Yugas

One of the most peculiar aspects of Hindu chronology is 'Yugas', vast time cycles. The current age, Kali Yuga, is said to last 432,000 years, and we're only about 5,000 years in!

Mom's Spit for Cleanliness in Nigeria

Among the Ewe people of Nigeria, a mother using her saliva to clean her child's face is not seen as unhygienic but as a gesture of love and care. This reflects a deep cultural understanding of maternal affection, surpassing notions of biological cleanliness.

Latah Culture-Linked Disorder
Found in some Malaysian and Indonesian cultures, Latah involves an exaggerated startle response, where individuals mimic the actions and speech of nearby people, sometimes uncontrollably.

Cosmic Cats
In 1963, France sent the first (and only) cat, Félicette, into space. Unlike many other animal astronauts, she successfully returned, contributing to early space science.

Floating Post Office
India has a floating post office on Dal Lake in Srinagar, Kashmir. Established in 2011, it operates as a post office and a museum, showcasing the importance of the extensive postal network in India.

Vertical Forests
In Milan, Italy, there's a pair of residential towers called Bosco Verticale (Vertical Forest) that are covered with over 20,000 trees and plants. These towers were designed to combat urban pollution and produce oxygen.

Giant Tortoise Gardens
On the Galápagos Islands, giant tortoises inadvertently assist in ecosystem restoration by dispersing seeds from the fruits they consume, helping forest areas regrow.

Non-Human Language
In the Torah, the Balaam's donkey is granted the power of speech by God, highlighting one instance of a non-human speaking a human language.

AI-Human Creativity Competitions
In 2018, an AI-generated painting titled "Portrait of Edmond de Belamy" was auctioned for over $432,000. The painting was created using a generative adversarial network (GAN), raising questions about AI's potential to challenge human creativity in art.

Disease Eradication
Researchers are exploring the use of genetic engineering to eradicate diseases such as malaria by genetically altering mosquitoes to render them incapable of transmitting the disease.

Old, Insecure Passwords

Despite countless warnings, "123456" and "password" consistently top the list of most common passwords, making them the easiest targets for hackers.

Space Dust Detection

Nano-detectors are being developed to identify individual particles of cosmic dust, which are inputs to understanding planetary formation and the origins of space materials.

Car Tires are Not All Black

Early car tires were white due to the natural color of rubber. The first black tires were produced when carbon black was added to improve durability and longevity.

Elephants' Intuition

Elephants can differentiate between human languages and run away from those more associated with poachers. This suggests a sophisticated understanding of human threats.

Cybercrime Economy

If cybercrime were a country, it would be the world's third-largest economy after the U.S. and China, with costs projected to exceed $10 trillion annually by 2025.

Fake Eggs for Real Change

Conservationists have used 3D-printed fake turtle eggs with embedded GPS trackers to combat poaching. The fake eggs travel along illegal trade routes, providing invaluable data.

Drokpa and Polyandry

The Drokpa community from the Himalayas practice polyandry, where a woman may have multiple husbands, often brothers. This practice is linked to keeping family land holdings intact and manageable.

No Snakes

There are no native snake species in New Zealand. While you might find sea snakes in the oceans, the land is blissfully snake-free.

Jabba the Hut Trap-Door Incident

In "Return of the Jedi," the actor who played the Gamorrean Guard accidentally fell through a trapdoor during filming, resulting in "greener" water under Jabba's palace—a mix-up in costume dyes.

The Voynich Manuscript Quandary

This mysterious illustrated codex, believed to have been created in the 15th century, contains text in an unknown language or script that has yet to be deciphered, intriguing cryptographers and archaeologists alike.

Email's Origin

The @ symbol used in email addresses was chosen to designate the user from the machine they were using on ARPANET, the precursor to the internet, because it wasn't a common symbol at the time and hence reduced confusion.

Fermented Fruit Anthology

Biogas technology allows us to convert food waste and fruit scraps into renewable energy. In Sweden, biogas from such sources is widely used to fuel public transport buses!

Stranded Apollo 12 Medallions

In the vastness of space, tiny medallions meant to honor fallen astronauts ended up strewn across the surface of the Moon after Apollo 12's launch left them behind.

Criminal Taxidermy

In the late 19th century, French police used life-sized taxidermy casts of criminal faces made from their death masks to create forensic libraries for criminal investigations.

Forced Sterilizations

Historical instances and some continuing practices of forced sterilizations on certain populations, often without consent or fair justification, highlight glaring ethical violations and issues of human rights.

Druids and Mistletoe

In ancient Celtic traditions, Druids held mistletoe in high esteem, particularly when found growing on oak trees. It was believed to have magical properties that could cure diseases, offer protection, and serve as an aphrodisiac.

Kosher Microwaves

Some strictly observant Jews have multiple microwaves in their kitchens to separately prepare dairy and meat dishes, adhering to the dietary laws of kashrut, which prohibit these food groups from being cooked or eaten together.

Octopus DNA

Research suggests that octopus DNA is remarkably complex and dramatically different from typical mollusks, showing a surprising amount of rearranged genomic elements referred to as "genomic islands of innovation."

Buddha Predicting Ages

In the Dhammapada, a popular scripture in Buddhism, there are teachings and stories which suggest that the Buddha lived for numerous past and future eons, reflecting on long cosmic cycles.

Frisbee's Pie Base

The Frisbee was invented after a group of students began throwing pie tins from the Frisbie Pie Company for fun. This informal game inspired the Wham-O toy company to create the plastic version we know today.

Himba Hair Art

In Namibia, the Himba tribe uses a special mixture of butterfat and ochre pigment to create intricate and symbolic hairstyles that convey age, status, and marital status. These hairstyles are strikingly distinctive and central to their identity.

Privacy Paradox

Surveys consistently reveal that while many people express concern over data privacy and wish for better protection, they often do not take precautionary steps to safeguard their own data.

One-line factoids, bizarre truths and juicy chunks of wisdom

Nanoshells for Cancer

Nanoshells, tiny beads of silica covered in gold, can be designed to absorb specific wavelengths of light and are being used in treating cancer by targeting tumors and destroying them with heat.

Synchronized Synchronizing Shrimp

The mantis shrimp uses a unique form of communication called "rapping," similar to a rhythmic knocking, which is both a mating call and territorial warning.

Blood Falls

In East Antarctica, there's the mysterious Blood Falls, where iron-rich, hypersaline water flows down a glacier, staining the ice red like blood.

The Ural "Singing" Rocks

Located in the Ural Mountains, these rocks are known for producing musical tones when struck, resulting from their unique composition of quartz and iron.

Epic Migrations

The Great Migration in the Serengeti involves over 1.5 million wildebeest, 200,000 zebras, and other animals making a 1,200-mile round trip across Tanzania and Kenya annually. It's one of the most spectacular wildlife shows on Earth.

Cow Manure Power

Manure from livestock can be used to produce biogas, a renewable energy source. Anaerobic digesters break down manure to produce methane, which can be turned into electricity or heat.

Cricket Fighting

The traditional Chinese pastime of cricket fighting has been popular for over a thousand years, with tournaments often attracting large audiences.

Quantum Zeno Effect

Frequent observation of a quantum system can inhibit its state from changing, effectively freezing its dynamics. It's named after Zeno's paradoxes, which deal with the idea that motion is an illusion.

Non-Newtonian Cornstarch

A mixture of cornstarch and water creates a "non-Newtonian fluid" called oobleck, which behaves like a solid if you punch it but flows like a liquid if you gently set it down.

Floating Farms

In densely populated places like Bangladesh, floating farms are gaining popularity. Bamboo rafts covered with soil grow crops, demonstrating innovative agricultural adaptation to flooding.

Underwater 'Waterfalls'

The Denmark Strait cataract, located between Greenland and Iceland, is the largest underwater waterfall on Earth. The drop is over 11,500 feet, which is more than three times the tallest waterfall on land.

Potato Chips by Accident

The popular potato chip was invented by accident in 1853 when Chef George Crum, frustrated by a customer's complaint about thick french fries, sliced them extremely thin, fried them to a crisp, and inadvertently created the first potato chip.

Testing Robots in Japan

Japan has experimented with robots as examiners in school tests. These robots evaluate the students' physical and technological skills alongside traditional academics.

Banach-Tarski Paradox

This theorem posits that you can theoretically break a sphere into a finite number of pieces and reassemble them into two identical spheres of the same size, relying on properties of infinity and non-measurable sets.

Phantom Limb Sensation

After losing a limb, some people still experience sensations, including pain, as if the limb were still there. This phenomenon is known as phantom limb syndrome and occurs because the brain continues to receive signals from nerves that originally served the missing limb.

Fluoride in Water Is Controversial

While heralded as one of the great public health achievements for reducing tooth decay, water fluoridation has also attracted conspiracy theories. Some opponents believe it to be a government mind-control plot, even though no scientific evidence supports these claims.

Hemingway's Cats with Extra Toes

Ernest Hemingway was a cat lover and owned a six-toed cat named Snow White. Today, the Hemingway Home in Key West is home to many descendants of Snow White, most of which also have the polydactyl trait.

Luk Thep Doll in Thailand

Some Thai people believe in "Luk Thep" dolls, known as "child angels," which are believed to be possessed by spirits that bring luck and fortune to their owners. These dolls are often cared for and pampered like real children.

J.R.R. Tolkien's Elaborate Languages

The depth of Tolkien's commitment to world-building in his works was so immense that he created multiple detailed languages for his Middle-earth books. Quenya and Sindarin, languages of the Elves, are particularly developed, complete with grammatical structures.

Designer Babies

The development of gene-editing technology opened up the possibility of creating "designer babies," where genetic modifications could alter traits - turning once science fiction ideas into real ethical discussions about genetic modification, consent, and societal impact.

Salto del Colacho in Spain

In Castrillo de Murcia, Spain, the "El Colacho" festival involves men dressed as the devil jumping over babies laid on mattresses in the street. This bizarre ritual is believed to cleanse the infants of sin and ensure they have a safe start to life.

Hot and Cold Green Power

There is a geothermal hybrid system in Iceland that not only harnesses the Earth's heat for energy but also uses the byproduct CO_2 for cultivating vegetables in nearby greenhouses.

Non-Locality

Quantum mechanics defies local realism; entangled particles exhibit correlations that cannot be explained by signals traveling at or below the speed of light, challenging classical intuitions about causality and locality.

Quantum Entanglement

Entangled particles share a connection so strong that the state of one instantly influences the state of another, no matter how far apart they are in the universe. Albert Einstein famously referred to this as "spooky action at a distance."

Christmas in Summer

Because Christmas falls in the Australian summer, it's common for Australians to celebrate with beach outings, barbecues, and water activities, contrasting the traditional winter holiday scenes elsewhere.

The Shower Hood (1970s)

This transparent plastic hood was made to keep hair dry in the shower. While functional, it was deemed too ridiculous for regular use.

Floating Motors

Amphibious vehicles that can traverse both land and water have been around since the early 20th century. During WWII, the German-designed Volkswagen Schwimmwagen was one of the most produced.

Algorithm Breaker

Quantum computing poses a significant threat to classical encryption algorithms. A sufficiently powerful quantum computer could break widely used encryption methods, like RSA, that are fundamental to internet security.

Cows on Virtual Reality

Israeli cows are among the most productive in the world, producing more milk per cow than anywhere else. Some have even experimented with VR headsets for cows to improve their well-being.

World's Longest Underwater Pipeline

The Nord Stream pipelines, stretching from Russia to Germany under the Baltic Sea, are among the longest underwater pipelines globally, traversing over 1,200 km (750 miles).

Ritual Finger Amputation

The Dani tribe in Papua, Indonesia, have a mourning practice where members cut off the top of a finger to express grief after the death of a relative. This act of severing a part of oneself is seen as a profound signal of loss and pain.

Sense of Smell

Women typically have a more acute sense of smell than men, which may be attributed to evolutionary roles in identifying healthy mates and food quality.

Sámi Reindeer Races

The indigenous Sámi people of northern Scandinavia host thrilling reindeer races on frozen lakes every winter, a spectacle full of speed and cultural significance.

First Hard Disk Had Minimal Storage

IBM's first hard disk drive was introduced in 1956 and could store just 5 MB of data. The drive was the size of a refrigerator and weighed over a ton.

Inca Quipus

The Incas used a sophisticated system called quipus for record-keeping. These were bundles of knotted cords used to convey information, yet their exact decoding remains only partially understood.

Ice Festival

The Harbin International Ice and Snow Sculpture Festival features gigantic structures made of ice blocks from the Songhua River, some up to 20 feet tall.

Temple of Rats

The Karni Mata Temple in Rajasthan is home to over 25,000 rats. These rats, considered sacred, freely roam the temple, and devotees try to spot the rare white rats as they are thought to bring good luck.

Euler's Number Everywhere

The number e (approximately 2.718) appears in calculations involving growth and decay, and it astonishingly shows up in unrelated areas such as probability, statistics, and even complex numbers.

The Betz Mystery Sphere

In 1974, the Betz family of Florida found a mysterious metal sphere on their property. When moved or touched, the sphere exhibited strange behaviors, such as sudden vibrations and directional rolling, but its origin or true purpose remains unknown.

Ocean Acidification's Effect

As oceans absorb more carbon dioxide from the atmosphere, pH levels decrease, leading to ocean acidification. This process can dissolve the shells of marine animals, particularly affecting species like corals and shellfish.

The Pollock Twins

In 1957, two sisters in England died in a car accident. A year later, their mother gave birth to twin girls who seemed to possess memories and birthmarks matching their deceased sisters, leading to speculation about reincarnation.

Lunar Influence on Personality

Many ancient cultures, including the Greeks and Romans, believed the moon influenced human behavior and personality, leading to the term "lunatic," suggesting madness purportedly caused by the moon's phases.

The University of Timbuktu

Timbuktu, in present-day Mali, was home to one of the world's first universities in the 12th century, attracting students from across Africa and the Middle East during its golden age.

The Vedic Flying Machines

Ancient Hindu texts like the Vaimanika Shastra describe flying machines called Vimanas, said to have been used thousands of years ago.

Human-Powered Energy

Some gyms have equipped exercise machines to harness the energy produced by individuals working out. This energy can be fed into the power grid or used to power the facility.

The Grauballe Man Mystery

The Grauballe Man, a bog body found in Denmark, is so well-preserved that his fingerprints remain intact. He died over 2,000 years ago, possibly as a sacrificial offering or because of a violent conflict.

Phoenician Dye

The Phoenicians extracted a luxury purple dye, Tyrian purple, from the glands of sea snails. This dye was highly prized and incredibly expensive, often associated with royalty and the elite.

Nuclear Shelter Preparedness

Switzerland has enough nuclear fallout shelters to house its entire population. Every resident is guaranteed a spot in the event of a nuclear disaster.

The Chaucerian Effect

Geoffrey Chaucer's "The Canterbury Tales" is known for popularizing the use of the English vernacular when Latin and French dominated literature, seen as bizarre at the time.

Weird Edibles

In China, you might find unusual items like seahorses, starfish, and scorpions skewered and sold at street food markets, reflecting a unique and adventurous food culture.

Risk-Taking Behavior

Men often take more risks than women, influenced by higher testosterone levels and societal factors encouraging bold behavior in men.

Flashbacks in VR

Studies have shown VR can help treat PTSD by exposing patients to controlled VR environments that help them process traumatic memories more healthily.

Rastafarian Ital Diet

Rastafarians follow an "Ital" diet, focusing on natural and pure food. Some observe strict rules against salt and processed foods, believing it's crucial for spiritual health.

The Oldest University

Al-Qarawiyyin University in Fez, Morocco, founded in 859 CE by a woman named Fatima al-Fihri, is considered one of the oldest continuously operating educational institutions in the world.

The Isdal Woman

In 1970, a woman's charred body was found in Norway's Isdalen Valley. Despite an extensive investigation, her identity and how she died were never definitively established, leading to endless speculation.

Graveyard for Ships

Namibia's Skeleton Coast is infamous for its treacherous fogs, violent surf, and shifting sands, making it a notorious "graveyard" for ships. It gets its name from the countless shipwrecks scattered along its shore.

Hair's On Fire

Human hair is virtually indestructible, except by flame. It doesn't deteriorate due to cold, change of climate, water, or other natural forces.

The Blurry Infinite

Hotel Infinity, imagined by mathematician David Hilbert, is a hotel with infinite rooms which can always accommodate more guests, illustrating the peculiar properties of infinite sets.

Poo Power

Human and animal waste can be converted into bioenergy. In the UK, some buses are powered by methane derived from sewage waste, cleverly dubbed "poo buses."

The Dark Web's Size

The so-called "Dark Web," where certain illicit activities occur, makes up only about 0.01% of the entire web, though it remains a persistent source of concern for its anonymity and hard-to-regulate nature.

Antiquity vs. Architecture

In Rome, strict urban planning laws ensure that any time construction digs deeper than 70 cm (27.5 inches), archaeologists must inspect and document findings to preserve the city's ancient heritage.

One-line factoids, bizarre truths and juicy chunks of wisdom

Cursing Mummy
The Curse of the Pharaohs is an alleged curse thought to be cast upon any person who disturbs the mummy of an Ancient Egyptian, especially a pharaoh. Notable real-life events connected to this belief include the untimely deaths of those who opened Tutankhamun's tomb.

Alien Hand Syndrome
People with this rare condition experience one of their hands acting independently from their thoughts and intent, seemingly possessing a mind of its own.

Phonemic Clicks
Southern African languages like Xhosa and Zulu are known for their click consonants, sounds that are rare in most other languages of the world.

Spiders Under Ice
Believe it or not, tiny ice spiders, known as "Paralopidium," are one of the few terrestrial animals that have adapted to survive in Antarctica's extreme conditions.

The Fountain of Sulfur
In the 1800s, vials of sulfuric acid were often opened in very cool shows. A small, hot iron was inserted into a flask, and when the stopper was removed, sulfuric acid would shoot out like a sulfur fountain.

Denmark's Freetown Christiania
This neighborhood in Copenhagen is an autonomous community with its own rules and culture. Founded in 1971, it is known for its artistic vibe and liberal attitudes, including the controversial "Green Light District" for cannabis.

Faster-than-Light Rotations
The outer regions of some black holes (ergospheres) twist spacetime so powerfully that anything there, including light, could appear to move in loops.

Ocean Currents Control Climate
The thermohaline circulation, often called the "global conveyor belt," moves vast amounts of ocean water across the globe, playing a crucial role in regulating Earth's climate by distributing heat.

Mouse Wasn't Always Famous

Despite being invented by Douglas Engelbart in the 1960s, the computer mouse didn't become widely used until the 1980s, when Apple included it with the Lisa computer.

Penguin Navigator

In 1996, NASA developed a unique VR system called "Antarctic explorer," which used VR to train astronauts by having them navigate a VR environment of Antarctica using a virtual penguin as their guide.

Marilyn Monroe and IQ

Despite her "dumb blonde" stereotype, Marilyn Monroe had an IQ of 168, which is reportedly higher than Albert Einstein's.

Physical Strength

Men generally have more muscle mass and physical strength due to higher levels of testosterone, but women often have greater muscle endurance and recovery capabilities.

Solar Freakin' Roadways

There are efforts to create solar panel roads that not only generate electricity but could also melt snow, provide lighting, and even have integrated pressure sensors to alert drivers to obstacles.

The Tamam Shud Case

In 1948, an unidentified man was found dead on Somerton Beach in Australia with a note saying "Tamam Shud" in his pocket, meaning "ended" in Persian. Despite numerous theories, his identity and cause of death remain a mystery.

Time and Language

The concept of time is expressed differently across languages; for example, Mandarin speakers might organize time vertically (younger events above older ones), whereas English speakers typically use a horizontal axis.

The Infamous $1 Billion Tweet

When Facebook acquired Instagram for $1 billion in 2012, Twitter considered but declined to purchase the app simply by missing the opportunity.

One-line factoids, bizarre truths and juicy chunks of wisdom

The Starving Poet
The French poet Gérard de Nerval famously walked a pet lobster on a leash through the streets of Paris. He claimed lobsters were "peaceful, serious creatures" who "know the secrets of the sea."

The Dancing Plague of 1518
In Strasbourg, France, in 1518, hundreds of people inexplicably began dancing uncontrollably for days. The cause of this so-called "dancing plague" remains a mystery, with theories ranging from mass hysteria to ergot poisoning.

Ancient Greek Daemon Spirits
In Greek mythology, "daemon" referred to a guiding spirit rather than evil beings as commonly interpreted today. These daemons were considered good spirits influencing people's fortunes and personalities.

The Strange Case of Art Therapy
In the 1940s, British artist Adrian Hill found out that creating art was beneficial during his tuberculosis treatment. He coined the term "art therapy," which led to its integration into mental health practices.

Quantum Tunneling
Particles can pass through solid barriers that would normally be insurmountable according to classical physics. This effect is essential in processes such as nuclear fusion in stars and is utilized in technologies like tunnel diodes and scanning tunneling microscopes.

Vanuatu Land Dives
On Pentecost Island in Vanuatu, the land diving ritual known as "Nagol" involves men leaping from tall wooden towers with only vines tied to their ankles to break their fall. This is considered a test of bravery and a precursor to modern bungee jumping.

The Sliced Bread Revolution
In the 1940s, during World War II, sliced bread was banned in the U.S. to conserve resources. This had a curious indirect effect on public health, as people had to use knives again, reportedly increasing butter and jam consumption.

The Walking Marriage of the Mosuo

The Mosuo people in China's Yunnan province are considered one of the last matrilineal societies. Though this fact pertains to Asia, it creates a striking parallel with the Himba people of Namibia, who also practice unique marriage customs that emphasize matrilineal ties.

The Panda's Thumb

Pandas have evolved a pseudo-thumb from a wrist bone which helps them grasp bamboo, their primary food source. This shows how evolution can repurpose structures for new functions.

Under Ice Lakes

Lake Vostok is the largest subglacial lake in Antarctica, buried beneath 4 kilometers (2.5 miles) of ice. It has been isolated for millions of years and may host unique microbiological life.

Biomimicry in Wind Turbines

Some wind turbine designs are inspired by the shape and movement of humpback whale fins, whose unique bumps, called tubercles, allow for increased lift and reduced drag.

The Matterhorn Croissant

The croissant, though typically associated with France, actually originates from the Austrian and Swiss Alps. The popular story suggests it was inspired by Alpine warriors resisting Ottoman sieges.

Marcel Duchamp's "Fountain"

In 1917, Marcel Duchamp submitted a urinal titled "Fountain" to an art exhibition as part of his readymade series. This act was highly controversial but crucial in challenging traditional notions of art, opening the doors to conceptual art.

Pythagorean Fear of Beans

The followers of the Greek philosopher Pythagoras abstained from eating beans. They believed beans contained the souls of the dead and avoided them due to a belief that beans and humans emerged from the same source of primordial ooze.

One-line factoids, bizarre truths and juicy chunks of wisdom

Bitcoin's Mysterious Founder
The creator of Bitcoin, known under the pseudonym Satoshi Nakamoto, remains unidentified to this day. The launching of Bitcoin in 2009 has dramatically changed how digital assets are perceived globally.

Cadaver Dogs' Sensitivity
Specially trained dogs can detect decomposed human remains buried up to 12 feet underground and can even discern cadaver scent in a body of water.

Uluru's Prohibition of Climbing
Climbing Uluru, a sacred Aboriginal site and landmark, was officially prohibited in 2019. The site is revered by the Indigenous Anangu people, and climbing it was discouraged for years before the outright ban.

Bedbug Battles
In some species of bedbugs, the males practice "traumatic insemination," where they pierce the female's abdominal wall with their genitalia, rather than using the reproductive tract.

The World's Longest Pizza Route
Sweden's famous "Pitepalt", a hearty potato dumpling, has an unofficial take-out adaptation that covers a 1,300-kilometer route, making it one of the longest pizza delivery routes in the world.

Daniel Radcliffe's Hair Art
The "Harry Potter" star once used his own hair to make art on a woman's bikini line for an MTV sketch with artist Jim Tavare.

Ear Prints
Just as unique as fingerprints, ear prints can sometimes be left behind at crime scenes and have been used as forensic evidence, especially in cases of burglaries.

Stamps as Money
In 1930s Austria, a small town issued its own currency using postage stamps during the Great Depression. This "stamp scrip" was created to keep the local economy moving by encouraging spending rather than saving.

Pink Dolphin Mystery

In the Amazon River, there are pink dolphins known as "boto." Local legends suggest they transform into handsome men at night to woo humans!

Living Mountains

In Ainu mythology, the native people of Japan believe that mountains can be alive. They talk about the kamuy (spirit) of mountains, which makes the earth and mountains living entities worthy of respect and offering.

The Case of Anna O

The first patient psychoanalyzed by Josef Breuer and Sigmund Freud, Anna O's treatment led to the development of talk therapy. Her case blurred lines between reality and fantasy, with dramatic symptom presentations.

Iceland's Elf Belief

In Iceland, a significant portion of the population believes in the existence of elves, or "huldufólk" (hidden people). Road construction projects have been altered to avoid disturbing their supposed habitats!

Supertasks

These are tasks that involve an infinite number of actions in a finite amount of time, creating paradoxes like "Thompson's Lamp," where a lamp is switched on and off in increasingly shorter intervals.

Dentistry of the Past

The ancient Egyptians practiced a rudimentary form of dentistry around 3000 BCE. Archaeological evidence shows they drilled teeth to remove decay and perhaps also performed extractions.

Brinicles - The Icy Finger of Death

In polar oceans, brinicles form beneath sea ice. These are underwater icicles that sink and freeze everything they touch, creating a deadly trap for bottom-dwelling sea creatures.

Monet's Eye Condition

Late in life, Claude Monet suffered from cataracts, which affected his perception of color. This influenced his artwork, leading to a noticeable shift in his color palette, often with redder and more yellow hues.

One-line factoids, bizarre truths and juicy chunks of wisdom

Social Structure
Dogs are pack animals with a hierarchical structure, which means they naturally follow a leader. Cats are more solitary and independent, often establishing their territory rather than social hierarchies.

Feral Camel Population
Australia has the world's largest population of feral camels, with numbers once estimated to be over a million. The camels roam the Outback and are descended from those brought over for transportation in the 19th century.

Fridge Mountain in the UK
In 2004, a bizarre piece of EU environmental legislation led to enormous piles of discarded fridges in the UK because they were waiting to have their CFC-containing insulation properly disposed of. This was due to a delay in the country's ability to meet the new EU standards.

Rocket Festival in Thailand and Laos
Before the annual monsoon rains, many in Northeast Thailand and Laos hold rocket festivals, or "Bun Bang Fai," where people build homemade rockets and launch them to encourage rains and symbolically communicate with sky deities.

Charybdis' Origin
The monstrous whirlpool in Greek mythology, Charybdis, was once a naiad. She was transformed into a sea monster by Zeus as punishment for helping her father, Poseidon, flood lands and steal oxen from Heracles.

Smiley Face Patent
In 1982, Scott Fahlman posted the original smiley face emoticon :-) on a bulletin board, marking the first documented use of emoticons. While not patented, it's notable how these tiny symbols have become part of digital communication.

Eco-Friendly Constitution
Ecuador became the first country in the world to recognize the rights of nature in its constitution in 2008, giving ecosystems the right to exist and persist.

Gravitational Waves
The collision of two black holes sends ripples through spacetime, known as gravitational waves, which have been detected here on Earth, opening a new way to observe the universe.

Underwater City
China's "Atlantis," the ancient city of Shi Cheng, lies submerged beneath Qiandao Lake. This city dates back to the second century and remains well-preserved.

Smell of Death
Forensic scientists are studying the complex odors emitted by decomposing bodies to develop sensors that can identify hidden graves based solely on smell.

The Village of Twins
Kodinhi, a village in Kerala, is famous for having an unusually high number of twins. With over 400 pairs of twins among its population, the phenomenon remains a mystery.

GDP Happiness Adjustments
Countries like Bhutan measure economic success not just by GDP, but by Gross National Happiness (GNH), taking into account spiritual and well-being factors.

Two Places at Once
The town of Baarle is split by the Belgium-Netherlands border with a surprising twist. In some places, homes and businesses have their front doors in different countries due to the complicated carve-up of the border.

Burning the Clocks in Semarang, Indonesia
Part of the Islamic New Year celebration locally known as "Tabuik," giant wood and bamboo clocks are paraded through the town before being ceremonially set ablaze, symbolizing letting go of time gone by.

One-line factoids, bizarre truths and juicy chunks of wisdom

Treatment
This treatment, in which growth attenuation is applied to severely disabled individuals to improve their quality of life, has been controversial, raising issues related to human rights and bodily autonomy of individuals unable to consent.

A Kiwi Road Warning
In an unusual homage to its kiwi birds, New Zealand has at times printed road safety bills featuring images of kiwis wearing reflective vests, urging drivers to be considerate of the nocturnal bird.

Italy's Love for Fireworks
Italians are credited with transforming simple fireworks into elaborate displays, adding artistry in both choreography and color effects during the Renaissance Period.

The Ötzi Effect
Ötzi the Iceman, a naturally mummified human from around 3300 BCE, was discovered in the Alps. Many researchers involved with him became subjects of urban legends about "Ötzi's Curse" due to a string of untimely deaths linked to the project.

Cat Flap Legislation
In the Swiss city of Waldenburg, it is mandatory by law to provide a cat flap in any new building to ensure access for cats, reflecting the country's strong animal welfare ethic.

The Flannan Isles Lighthouse Disappearance
In 1900, three lighthouse keepers vanished from the Flannan Isles off the coast of Scotland without a trace. Theories about their disappearance include freak waves, a ghost ship, and even alien abduction.

Reduplicative Paramnesia
This disorder involves the belief that a place or location has been duplicated and exists simultaneously in two or more locations.

Virtual Celebrities
In Japan, some virtual reality idols like Hatsune Miku have gained such popularity that they hold entire concerts in VR. These digital characters even have dedicated fan followings, as if they were real celebrities.

Upside-Down Mezuzah

In some homes, you may notice that the mezuzah (a small case affixed to the doorframe containing a parchment with Hebrew verses) is slanted. This is a compromise between two historical rabbinic opinions on whether it should be vertical or horizontal.

The Banana Slug's Love Dart

Banana slugs have a peculiar mating ritual that includes chewing off each other's penises after copulation. However, they're hermaphrodites, so they can continue to reproduce even after losing their male organ.

Oulipo Group

Founded in 1960, a group known as Oulipo (Ouvroir de littérature potentielle) created poetry using complex mathematical and combinatorial structures. They sought to invent new literary forms by applying rigid rules, like writing without using the letter "E."

Spaghettification

If you fell into a black hole, you would experience "spaghettification." The intense gravitational forces would stretch you long and thin, like spaghetti.

The Small-World Experiment

Conducted by Stanley Milgram, this experiment led to the concept of "six degrees of separation," suggesting that everyone in the world is connected to everyone else by six or fewer social connections.

Matzo Penalty Shootout

During Passover, the matzo's reputation as the "bread of affliction" leads to creative uses like matzo sports tournaments in some communities, showcasing how this staple can even become a whimsical part of cultural activities.

Bamboo and Exploding Rocks

When heated, certain rocks can trap water inside and cause steam to build up until they explode. Historically, this was one reason early miners used to believe rocks were "alive."

Twitter's Origin as a Podcast Platform
Twitter was initially conceived as a podcasting platform called Odeo. After Apple launched iTunes' podcast platform, Twitter pivoted to become a microblogging service due to dwindling demand for Odeo's original format.

Sound Frequency
Cats can hear ultrasonic sounds up to 65 kHz, which is higher than dogs, who can hear frequencies up to 45 kHz. This ability is useful for detecting the chattering of rodents.

Timbuktu's Misplaced Reputation
Once a rich hub of learning and commerce in the Malian Empire, European maps of the 19th century often placed Timbuktu in the wrong location, contributing to its mysterious lore as a city of gold.

The Treadmill Bike (2012)
A combination of a treadmill and a bicycle, this invention meant you could walk on it while on the move. Its unwieldy nature prevented it from becoming a common sight.

No Central Authority
Unlike some religions, Islam does not have a single central religious authority, leading to a diverse set of interpretations and practices across different cultures.

Vampire Numbers
These are numbers with an even number of digits that can be factored into two numbers, called "fangs," which together use all the original digits. For example, $1260 = 21 \times 60$.

The Human Echo
The Mbuti Pygmies from the Democratic Republic of the Congo are renowned for their unique musical practices, which include "vocal-phasing"—this involves echoed singing that mimics the densely layered sounds of their forest environment.

Kangaroo Courtship
Male kangaroos flex their muscles and perform elaborate poses to attract females during mating season. Their large biceps are not just for combat but also to impress potential mates.

Bird Celebrities
New Zealand has a rich avian celebrity culture with birds like the kakapo and kiwi capturing global attention. The kakapo, a flightless parrot that's also nocturnal, was crowned "Bird of the Year" multiple times in conservation awareness campaigns.

Bald Haircuts
In the Haredi Jewish community, certain women shave their heads after marriage and wear wigs (sheitels) as part of their religious and cultural practice.

Zombie Companies
"Zombie companies" are those that can barely cover the interest on their debt but not the debt itself. These firms linger in the economy, often propped up by low-interest rates, without making any real profit or progress.

Bioluminescent Bays
There are water bodies like Mosquito Bay in Puerto Rico that are so densely populated with bioluminescent organisms, primarily dinoflagellates, that they glow intensely at night when disturbed. This eerie glow has earned such locations the nickname "Bio Bays."

Eco-Friendly Elections
In Finland, political candidates must file an environmental report after elections, detailing the environmental impact of their campaigns. This includes everything from energy consumption to the sustainability of campaign materials.

Nose Prints
Similar to human fingerprints, a dog's nose print is unique to each individual. Meanwhile, even though cats' nose prints can be similar, it's not commonly used for identification.

One-line factoids, bizarre truths and juicy chunks of wisdom

The Dead Sea Phenomenon

The Dead Sea, bordered by Israel, is the world's saltiest body of water that allows you to float effortlessly without sinking. Its mineral-rich mud is also said to possess health benefits.

Tree Castles

In Ethiopia, urban planners built a city called Hawassa that uses infrastructure made from living tree roots. Bridges, and even some parts of buildings, are created using intertwining roots for support.

Moon Tastes Like Gunpowder

According to astronauts, the Moon dust smells and tastes like gunpowder. This is due to the high reactivity of the Moon's surface particles when exposed to humid, oxygen-rich environments like those inside the space suits.

Tap Water Coin Toss

In 2017, a flight was delayed after an elderly passenger tossed coins into an airplane engine for "good luck," revealing a widespread belief in fortune through coin tossing.

Perpetual Potatoes

The International Potato Center in Peru holds the largest collection of potato diversity with over 4,500 different varieties, crucial for breeding pest-resistant and drought-resistant strains.

Beer Pong Diplomacy

In 1971, an American ping pong team was invited to visit China, which contributed to thawing Cold War tensions and establishing informal diplomatic relations. This event is often called "ping pong diplomacy."

United Kingdom

Law states that it's illegal to handle a salmon suspiciously. This is actually part of the Salmon Act of 1986, meant to curtail illegal fishing practices.

Mist-ery Energy

Researchers are investigating how to generate power from the energy produced by water droplets hitting a surface, harnessing the principles of static electricity.

The Impact of Miasma Theory

For centuries, European health interventions were based on the miasma theory, which held that diseases were spread by "bad air." This belief delayed significant advances in understanding germ theory but also led to better sanitation practices.

Japanese Haiku

The haiku is a form of Japanese poetry that traditionally captures fleeting moments in just three lines of 5, 7, and 5 syllables. It is a deeply meditative and observational form emphasizing simplicity.

Secret Meteorite Collection

Thanks to its white icy surface, dark meteorites are easily visible. Antarctica is a prime location for finding meteorites. Over 20,000 have been collected for study, providing valuable insights into space.

The Origin of Car Horns

Before car horns, early automobiles were fitted with bells, whistles, or bulb horns. The modern electric car horn wasn't widely adopted until the early 20th century.

Agatha Christie's Mysterious Disappearance

In 1926, mystery writer Agatha Christie disappeared for 11 days, sparking a nationwide manhunt in England. She was eventually found staying at a hotel, registered under the name of her husband's mistress.

Whisker Communication

Cats have such sensitive whiskers that they can detect changes in the environment, like shifts in air currents, while dogs rely more on their sense of smell and hearing for environmental cues.

Ghost Cities

China has several "ghost cities" which are fully developed urban areas with hardly any residents, built in anticipation of future demand.

Dancing Plague of 1518

In Strasbourg, hundreds of people danced uncontrollably for days. This phenomenon, called choreomania, is still unexplained but thought to be a form of mass psychogenic illness, highlighting the mind's powerful reactions to stress and hysteria.

The Dyatlov Pass Incident
In 1959, nine experienced Russian hikers died mysteriously in the Ural Mountains. Their tent was found ripped from the inside, and the bodies exhibited baffling injuries. The cause of their deaths is still debated and unexplained.

Firework Testing Center
The Arabian desert, with its vast, open, and uninhabited spaces, is often used for testing fireworks—large displays are tested here well ahead of major international events.

Longest Name of A Place
New Zealand is home to the world's longest place name: Taumatawhakatangihangakoauauotamateapokaiwhenuakitanatahu. It refers to a hill in the Hawke's Bay region.

A Lake The Size Of Singapore
Lake Taupo is New Zealand's largest lake and even bigger than the entire city-state of Singapore.

Bleeding Statue
In the Italian town of Civitavecchia, a statuette of the Virgin Mary allegedly wept blood in 1995. This event drew widespread attention and pilgrimage despite ongoing debates about its authenticity.

The Hinterkaifeck Murders
In 1922, an entire family living on a farm in Bavaria was brutally murdered with a mattock. Oddly, it seemed the murderer stayed at the farm for several days afterward, feeding the animals. The case remains unsolved.

World Record for Largest Firework
The largest recorded firework shell designed was launched in Steamboat Springs, Colorado, in 2020. It weighed 2,797 pounds and shattered the previous record from the United Arab Emirates.

Stendhal Syndrome
Overwhelming and intense emotional responses, such as panic attacks, confusion, or hallucinations, can occur when exposed to art or natural beauty, particularly when surrounded by numerous masterpieces.

Reading Facial Expressions
Women typically excel over men in reading facial expressions and emotions, attributed to both biological factors and social conditioning.

Salty Reservoir
Your body has enough salt to fill a 3-pound box. It's the same amount of salt in about 28 McDonald's salt packets!

Anti-Gravity Hills
At Magnetic Hill near Leh in Ladakh, cars appear to roll uphill when parked on a specific spot. The phenomenon is actually an optical illusion caused by the surrounding landscape.

Algae as Fuel
Algae may hold the key to producing biofuels. Certain types of algae can be converted into oil, which can be refined into biodiesel, offering a promising alternative to fossil fuels.

Banana Radioactivity
Bananas contain potassium-40, a radioactive isotope. This makes them slightly radioactive, but don't worry — you'd have to eat millions of bananas in a short time to be affected.

Tuned-up "Astromechs"
In order to make the droids like R2-D2 sound more organic, sound designer Ben Burtt manipulated synthesized sounds with actual recordings of babies to create R2-D2's vocalizations.

Songdo International Business District
Built from the ground up near South Korea's Seoul, it's a "smart" city designed with sensors and data analytics that control everything from traffic to energy usage in real-time.

World's Smallest Roadworthy Car
The smallest car ever created was the Peel P50. At 54 inches long and 39 inches wide, it is the size of a suitcase and can fit only one adult.

The Schizophrenic Doppelgänger

In 1795, a German psychiatrist named Johann Christian Reil coined the term "schizophrenia," inspired by a case where a patient believed he had an invisible twin. This idea led to exploring the concept of dual consciousness.

Deep-Sea Gigantism

Many deep-sea creatures, like the giant isopod, grow to enormous sizes compared to their shallow-water relatives due to factors such as temperature, pressure, and slow metabolism rates in the deep ocean.

Antarctica's Unique Environmental Laws

The Antarctic Treaty, signed in 1959 and effective since 1961, designates Antarctica as a natural reserve devoted to peace and science. It places strict limits on human activity, including a ban on mining and military operations.

Bizarre Legality

There is no native human population, and several countries claim portions of the continent under the Antarctic Treaty System, which prohibits military activity, mineral mining, and supports scientific research.

Longest Single Verse

The longest verse in the Qur'an is Surah Al-Baqarah, Ayah 282, which is about 15 lines long and deals with financial transactions, underscoring the detail provided in religious texts regarding daily life.

Christopher Walken Was a Lion Tamer

As a teenager, Walken joined a circus and worked as an assistant lion tamer.

Sneeze Stallions

A sneeze can travel as fast as 100 miles per hour and can send 100,000 germs into the air.

Velcro from Nature

Swiss engineer George de Mestral invented Velcro after noticing how burdock burrs stuck to his dog's fur during a walk. The design inspired hook-and-loop fasteners now used in many industries.

Ford's Soybean Car

In 1941, Henry Ford made a car with a body built from a plastic using soybean derivatives. It was lighter than metal cars but didn't make it to mass production due to World War II.

Vocalization Variety

Dogs have about 10 different vocal sounds, whereas cats are true linguistic specialists with over 100 different sounds they can produce, allowing them a wide variety of vocal expressions.

Time Reversibility

At the quantum level, the fundamental laws of physics are time-symmetric. This means that in principle, quantum processes can run equally well forward or backward in time, leading to intriguing possibilities in theoretical physics.

Chinese Room

Philosopher John Searle's thought experiment argues against strong AI. It involves a person in a room following instructions to manipulate Chinese symbols without understanding; it's meant to show that computers can't "understand."

Longest Wall in the World

The Great Wall of China, built over several dynasties, stretches over 13,000 miles, making it the longest wall in the world.

Salt as Salary

The word "salary" comes from the Latin word "salarium," which means payment made to a Roman soldier for the purchase of salt, highlighting salt's historical economic value.

Bee's Fatalized Flight

When a male honeybee mates with the queen, his reproductive organ explodes and remains inside her, which ensures she remains fertilized with his genes. Unfortunately, the male dies shortly afterward.

Sand and Salt

The white sands of Crait in "The Last Jedi" were actually created using regular table salt for enhancing the landscape's effect, reportedly causing unexpected traction issues for the crew walking on set.

Taste Buds

Cats can't taste sweetness, which might explain why they are often disinterested in sugary treats. Dogs, on the other hand, have a broader range of taste buds and can enjoy sweet flavors.

Divine Lightning

In 1954, a stone gargoyle was struck by lightning at York Minster in England, causing a fire. Remarkably, another lightning strike happened in 1984, on the exact anniversary of a bishop accused of heresy in the English Reformation.

The Green Party's Roots

The world's first Green Party was established in Australia in 1972 as the United Tasmania Group, initiated over concerns about the damming of Lake Pedder.

Tom Cruise's Major Height Hack

Known for his action roles, Tom Cruise is actually 5'7" but often appears taller in movies through clever camera work and shoe lifts.

Ban on Hobby Growing

It is illegal in Switzerland to keep just one guinea pig or rabbit because they are social animals and can suffer from loneliness without companions. If one dies, you can rent a second one.

Marriage Contracts

In ancient Mesopotamia, couples entered into legally binding marriage contracts. These contracts dictated the bride's duties, dowry, and even potential penalties for divorce or infidelity.

Lakes that Sparkle

Tanzania's Lake Natron is known for its eerily reflective waters, which are also naturally caustic due to high levels of natron, a sodium carbonate. The lake's unique qualities give it a blood-red hue and can quickly calcify any animal that perishes in it.

The Living Bridges of India
In the Indian state of Meghalaya, the Khasi people have developed living bridges made from the roots of trees. These root bridges are not only an engineering marvel but also a perfect harmony of human and natural interaction, taking decades to grow.

SynBio 'New Life Forms'
Synthetic biology has created microorganisms with entirely synthetic DNA sequences, opening the door to "new life forms" tailored for specific functions, such as biofuel production.

The Rongorongo Scripts of Easter Island
Easter Island is known for its massive moai statues, but it also has ancient wooden tablets inscribed with the mysterious Rongorongo script. No one has successfully deciphered this script, leaving its meaning and origin unknown.

Quantum Vacuum Fluctuations
Even in a vacuum, there are temporary changes in the amount of energy, resulting in the spontaneous creation and annihilation of particle-antiparticle pairs. This phenomenon is a crucial part of quantum field theory.

Diverse Shinto Shrines
In Japan, Shintoism reveres countless kami (spirits), and some shrines are dedicated to unusual entities, including one for the spirit of matches and another for kitchen knives.

Singapore's Character and Citizenship Education
Singapore implemented a comprehensive Character and Citizenship Education (CCE) program, emphasizing values and ethics alongside academics, preparing students not just as individuals in a workforce but as engaged citizens.

Drop Bears
Australians often jest about dangerous creatures called *drop bears* — fictional koala-like creatures that supposedly drop from trees onto unsuspecting passersby and scratch their faces. It's a long-running practical joke on tourists. The way to keep the drop bears away is to put vegemite behind one's ears.

One-line factoids, bizarre truths and juicy chunks of wisdom

Dusty Origins
Most of the dust in your home is actually made up of dead human skin cells. You shed about 1.5 pounds of skin every year!

Duchamp's Alter Ego
Marcel Duchamp had a female alter ego named Rrose Sélavy, which he used to sign some of his artworks. This playful pseudonym was a pun on the French phrase "Eros, c'est la vie," meaning "Eros, that's life."

Coral IVF
In an effort to save coral reefs, scientists have developed methods of spawning corals in labs, releasing millions of coral larvae into the sea to repopulate damaged areas.

Jane Austen's Gold Ring
In the early 1800s, Jane Austen owned a rare and distinctive turquoise ring. What's interesting is that when the ring was auctioned in 2012, musician Kelly Clarkson purchased it. It took a government export ban to keep the ring in the UK as a cultural artifact.

No name for a pig
In France you cannot name a pig "Napoleon." This law protects the former emperor's name from being associated with an animal.

Beethoven's Unusual Compositions
Ludwig van Beethoven composed much of his iconic music while completely deaf. Perhaps stranger still, he was known to dip his head in cold water before composing to help stimulate his creativity.

Waves to Electricity
Wave energy converters capture the energy of ocean waves and transform it into electricity. This technology holds the potential for a reliable and consistent energy source as water covers over 70% of the earth's surface.

Volcanic Mailboxes in Iceland
Reykjavík, the capital of Iceland, has mail boxes in some of its volcanic craters, where tourists and locals can mail special "lava-themed" postcards.

Error Correction Challenges

Quantum computers are extremely sensitive to their environment, and maintaining their quantum states requires sophisticated error correction schemes. A quantum bit state can be altered just by a random slight disturbance, like a stray photon.

Carrot Power

Carrots were originally purple or white. The familiar orange variety was cultivated in the Netherlands in the 17th century to honor the royal House of Orange.

Yoda's Original Name

Before settling on "Yoda," the wise Jedi Master was originally named "Buffy" in early drafts. He was later referred to as "Minch Yoda."

Animal Deities

Animals like cows, monkeys, elephants (Lord Ganesha), snakes (Naga), and many others are venerated, and sometimes considered to be earthly forms of deities themselves.

Russian Language's Shared Word "Sputnik"

The word "sputnik" translates to "traveling companion," and gained international fame as the name of the first artificial Earth satellite launched by the Soviet Union in 1957.

The Walking Sleeping Bag (1972)

A sleeping bag with leg and arm slots allowing movement. Despite being practical, it was too cumbersome and odd to appeal to most campers.

Salpetriere's Hypnosis Shows

In the late 1800s, Jean-Martin Charcot performed public hypnosis demonstrations in Paris, blending entertainment with scientific inquiry, and advancing the study of hysteria.

A 15-Year Typo

The programming language called "FORTRAN" was intended to be named "Formula Translator." However, a typo from the early days stuck and became the official name.

Jerusalem's Street WiFi
Jerusalem offers free WiFi across the city, allowing anyone to stay connected while exploring its ancient streets.

Instant Martyrdom
St. Expeditus, the patron saint of procrastinators and emergencies, became an instant martyr according to legend. When he decided to convert, the devil appeared as a crow telling him to delay. He refused, killing the bird with a held cross, exclaiming "Hodie" ("Today").

Supermassive Black Holes
At the center of nearly every galaxy, including our own Milky Way, resides a supermassive black hole, containing millions to billions of times the mass of our Sun.

Pig Orgasms
Male pigs can have orgasms lasting up to 30 minutes, which is significantly longer than most other mammals.

Millions of Deities
Hinduism boasts an astonishing number of deities, with estimates ranging from 33 million to an infinite number, each with distinct roles and stories.

Tongkonan of the Torajan in Indonesia
The Tongkonan are traditional houses of the Toraja people, deeply symbolic and built on stilts with massive peaked roofs. Each serves an extended family, reflecting their ancestry and communal importance.

Concrete Poetry
In this visual form, the arrangement of the text on the page often forms a shape or image, further enhancing the poem's meaning—words form patterns, pictures, or shapes complementing the text.

Earth's Lowest Temperature
The coldest temperature ever recorded on Earth was in Antarctica: a bone-chilling minus 128.6 degrees Fahrenheit (minus 89.2 degrees Celsius) at the Soviet Union's Vostok Station in 1983.

The Voynich Manuscript

This mysterious manuscript, written in an unknown script and illustrated with strange plant and astronomical drawings, dates back to the 15th century. Despite the efforts of many cryptographers and linguists, its language and purpose remain a mystery.

Mount Kailash Mystery

Mount Kailash in Tibet is considered the abode of Lord Shiva, one of the principal deities in Hinduism. Interestingly, no human has ever successfully climbed to its peak, as it's regarded as a sacred and untouchable mountain.

Giraffe Varsity

The only known population of wild giraffes that swim exists on the plains of St. Lucia Estuary, South Africa. These giraffes have been observed swimming during flooding to move between islands.

Glow-in-the-Dark Animals

Scientists have used genetic engineering to create glow-in-the-dark animals. By inserting jellyfish genes into the DNA of pigs, fish, and even cats, researchers have created organisms that emit a greenish glow under blue or UV light.

The Boy in the Box

In 1957, the body of a young boy was found in a box in Philadelphia. Despite media attention and investigation, his identity and the circumstances of his death are still unknown.

Universal Nostratic Hypothesis

This unproven theory suggests that many of the world's language families, including Indo-European, Afro-Asiatic, and Uralic, stem from a single ancestral proto-language.

The Inaccurate Maps of the African Interior

Until the late 19th century, maps of Africa were notoriously inaccurate. It wasn't until European exploration in the 1800s that the rivers, mountains, and lakes of Africa were documented with any precision.

Koranic Repetition

In the Quran, the phrase "Bismillah hir Rahman ir Rahim" ("In the name of God, the Most Gracious, the Most Merciful") prefaces 113 of the 114 chapters (suras), emphasizing the centrality of God's mercy in Islam.

Entanglement

When qubits become entangled, the state of one qubit is directly related to the state of another, no matter the distance between them. This phenomenon baffled even Einstein, who referred to it as "spooky action at a distance."

Paved in Pink

In Vila Nova de Gaia, Portugal, entire streets were painted pink in an anti-heating initiative to reflect sunlight and reduce the urban heat island effect.

Palindrome Poem

One of the most unconventional forms of poetry is the palindrome poem, where the poem reads the same forwards and backwards. Composing such pieces is incredibly challenging due to the constraints on word choice and structure. For example: *A man, a plan, a canal: Panama.*

Netherlands' Bicycle Revolution

To combat pollution and as part of environmental policy initiatives in the 1970s, the Dutch government invested heavily in biking infrastructure, now giving the Netherlands one of the most cycle-friendly communities in the world.

Brahms' Beard

In his later years, Johannes Brahms grew a long, bushy beard, reportedly to avoid being recognized on the street. It became a signature part of his image.

The "Wilhelm Scream" Phenomenon

The Wilhelm Scream is a stock sound effect that has been used in hundreds of films since 1951. Originally recorded for the movie "Distant Drums", it's become an inside joke among sound editors.

Living with Corpses
The Aghori sect, a small group of ascetic Shaiva sadhus, often lives in cremation grounds and occasionally meditating with human remains, as they seek to transcend societal norms and discard human taboos.

Elders' Day
China legally enforces filial piety, where it's mandated by law for citizens to visit their elderly parents regularly.

Monkey King's Woes
In Chinese mythology, Sun Wukong, the Monkey King from "Journey to the West," is a trickster figure with incredible abilities. Despite his prowess, he is trapped under a mountain for 500 years due to his rebellious acts against heaven.

Cats Galore
Tel Aviv is sometimes referred to as the "cat capital" of the world due to its large population of street cats. They are so common that there are organizations and individuals dedicated to feeding and looking after them.

Zebra Crossings
No two zebras have the same pattern of stripes. Their unique patterns serve as identification, much like human fingerprints.

France and Spain's Wandering Borders
The Pheasant Island in the Bidasoa River alternates sovereignty every six months between France and Spain due to the Treaty of the Pyrenees of 1659.

Mind Uploading
Science fiction? Maybe not entirely philosophical thinking explores the implications of transferring human consciousness to computers, raising bizarre questions about identity, mortality, and rights of digital selves.

Firework Origins
Fireworks were invented in China around 2,000 years ago. They were accidently discovered by a Chinese cook who mixed sulfur, charcoal, and saltpeter (potassium nitrate).

One-line factoids, bizarre truths and juicy chunks of wisdom

Doppelgänger Domains
A crafty form of cyberattack involves creating domains that resemble legitimate ones by using subtly different characters (e.g., "go0gle.com" instead of "google.com"). These are often used in phishing scams.

The Taos Hum
In the small town of Taos, New Mexico, residents and visitors have reported hearing a mysterious low-frequency hum since the early 1990s. Despite numerous investigations, the source of the sound remains unknown.

Moonlit Madness
Mating activity in many coral reef creatures is triggered by lunar cycles, where spawning is synchronized with the full moon for effective fertilization.

Tidal Power Tsunami
The concept of using underwater "kites" to harness tidal energy is being explored. These kites can capture energy efficiently in slower currents, opening new frontiers for tidal power.

Wave-Particle Duality
In quantum mechanics, particles such as electrons and photons can exhibit both particle-like and wave-like behavior. This means that under certain conditions, particles can interfere and diffract like waves, yet still have distinct particle properties.

The Bermuda Triangle's Folklore
Known for mysterious disappearances, its geographical reputation mostly stems from folklore and myth rather than historical records. The region is one of the most heavily traveled shipping lanes in the world without unusual incidents compared to other regions.